What We Mean by Religion

WHAT
WE MEAN BY
RELIGION

~~~~~~~~~~~~~~~~~~~~~~~~~~~~~~~~~~

by

WILLARD L. SPERRY

~~~~~~~~~~~~~~~~~~~~~~~~~~~~~~~~~~

Essay Index Reprint Series

BOOKS FOR LIBRARIES PRESS
FREEPORT, NEW YORK

INTERNATIONAL STANDARD BOOK NUMBER:
0-8369-2370-7

LIBRARY OF CONGRESS CATALOG CARD NUMBER:
78-128316

PRINTED IN THE UNITED STATES OF AMERICA

Contents

Foreword

Florida Southern College Lectures

THIS VOLUME INITIATES A SERIES OF LECTURES ON RE-
LIGION TO BE GIVEN ANNUALLY AT FLORIDA SOUTHERN
College. Supplementing the regular classroom instruc-
tion in the subject, they emphasize the purpose of the
College to make religion an essential element in a
liberal education.

These lectures were delivered before the student
body and the public on March 14-19, 1940.

LUDD M. SPIVEY, *President*
Florida Southern College
Lakeland, Florida

What We Mean by Religion

Chapter I

RELIGION

WE ARE PLEDGED IN THESE PAGES TO THINK ABOUT FIVE
FAMILIAR WORDS: RELIGION, FAITH, PRAYER, MORALS,
GOD.

In any language the hard words to define are not
the long words which have been manufactured at a
late date; they are the old words that have been there
from the first—elemental words like "life, love, work."
Indeed the simpler the word the harder it will be to
define since it was born as a living thing out of man's
primal feelings, rather than assembled as a machine-
made product of reflective thought. If you know its
derivation the word "telephone" gives you no trouble;
it is "the voice from a distance." But who shall say
what the word "love" means and all that it means?

The formal definitions of such words are little more
than "nets to catch the wind." You have no sooner
captured them than they give you the slip and are free
again. The meshes of your net are too coarse to hold
them. A modern writer has put the case well:

The proper meaning of a word (I speak not of technical
terms, which kindly godparents furnish soon after birth
with neat and tidy definitions, but of words in a living

1

language) is never something upon which the word sits perched like a gull on a stone; it is something over which the word hovers like a gull over a ship's stern. Trying to fix the proper meaning in our minds is like trying to coax the gull to settle in the rigging, with the rule that the gull must be alive when it settles: one must not shoot it and tie it there.[1]

Therefore I am not proposing to try to define the words which are to be our themes. At the most I shall venture descriptions of them, one by one, as a man wandering around the foot of a mountain might sketch its changing contours seen from different angles. Perhaps the sum of these impressions may give us some intimation of the meaning of the whole word. But even so, we must accept the prospect that its total outline can never be seen from one place at one time; and from any given point of vantage its slopes will often be obscured by marching mists and its summit hidden in cloud.

I

The first of our words, then, is "religion." Let us begin by admitting that, as "no man hath seen God at any time," so no man has ever seen religion. This is an abstract word which we have coined for our convenience, to indicate certain of our ideas, emotions, attitudes, situations, acts, which seem to have a common

[1] R. G. Collingwood, *The Principles of Art* (London: Clarendon Press, 1938), p. 7.

recurring quality that warrants our bracketing them under a single head. When you go out to Stonehenge on Salisbury Plain and stand in the center of that silent circle of monoliths, you have a ghostly sense of ancient men peopling the scene for a transaction which you can only call religious.

> Above these fields a spirit broods,
> A sense of many watchers muttering near
> Of the lone Downland . . .
>
> A muttering from beyond the veils of Death
> From long dead men.

You know instinctively—to use Novalis' phrase—that those gray stones "bake no bread." They were the site for some act of worship or sacrifice, the details of which are lost in the dark backward and abysm of time.

We are met here by a stubborn problem, familiar to all students of philosophy, as to whether abstract nouns have any direct connection with reality, or whether they are the dead ends of hollow caves of thought, where we get only the echoes of what is real. That issue has never been settled, perhaps it never can be settled. But the fact that there is known to be a problem here should at least put us on our guard. The truth is that we never see religion as such—or Christianity for that matter; what we see is Savonarola on his fiery platform in Florence; and in response to the bishop's formula, "I separate thee from the church militant and triumphant," we hear Savonarola's reply, "Not from the church triumphant; that is beyond thy power." To such a situation we give the only word that is relevant and adequate, religion.

We shall be well advised, then, to preface what we have to say in these pages by a warning against the worship of abstract nouns. The heathen in his blindness—so runs the old hymn—bows down to wood and stone. So-called civilized man has collected these heathen idols and put them in his museums where he may smile at them, but he has not yet outgrown idolatry. John Calvin once said, cannily, that "the human heart is a perpetual forge of idols," and the modern world sometimes seems to be a busy workshop intent on turning out a host of abstract words which serve earth's many tribes as totem poles— words like capitalism, socialism, communism, liberalism, fascism, totalitarianism. These words have the power of rousing in our minds and hearts the fears and the fanatical devotion which have always attended idolatry. We cannot think and speak today without using such words; but we shall do well to realize that they serve us best when they are employed as signposts to help us find our way around the map of life rather than as idols before which we must prostrate ourselves.

The word "religion" in English speech has come, only later rather than earlier, to have the meaning which we now most commonly attach to it. As employed in Middle English it connoted membership in one or another of the orders of the pre-Reformation Church. Indeed, in modern Catholic usage, that meaning still survives in the adjective, used as a substantive, by which "a religious" is understood to be, let us say, a Benedictine or a Franciscan. Even in the eighteenth century Horace Walpole could say that his father had "retired into religion," entered a Catholic monastery.

The dictionary tells us that the origin of the word is obscure. Plainly it was lifted direct from the Latin noun *religio*, and that noun came in turn from a verb. Probably it came from the verb *religare*—to bind. Roman *religio* involved a recognized set of scruples and binding observances. It is this idea of formal obligation that carried over from Latin into English and suggested the earliest use of the word to connote membership in a monastic order with its vows, strict rules and fixed ceremonies. It was not until the sixteenth century, and the time of the Protestant Reformation, that the word was freed from its Catholic setting and released to serve as the name given to man's belief in a divine being and to the acts following that belief. The Oxford Dictionary gives the year 1535 as the earliest date at which the word "religion" was thus used in what is now to us its most familiar form.

The major religions of the world are of long standing in history. There has been no new religion of the first magnitude since the birth of Mohammedanism in the seventh century. It is a striking fact that with all our modern discoveries we have been so lacking in the power to "invent" a new religion, and that we are still so dependent on the distant past. Meanwhile, in spite of the threadbare report which is spread abroad in every time and place, that religion is dying before men's eyes, the world's historic religions have proved to have a vitality beyond all expectation. We can only conclude that, if they were wholly irrelevant to man's needs and wholly false to his world, they would have passed away long ago. We must believe that their amazing will to live is something more than a professional conspiracy of priests; that it has its roots in man's nature and needs and his place in the universe. Were there no such correspondence to experience the great religions of the world must have died of their own irrelevancy or have been put to death by dispassionate criticism. So, for example, when I see the Lord's Supper spread upon its Table, I am always made aware of the sheer survival power of this symbol over twenty centuries. The Sacrament has meant many different things to many men in many ages and places. A vast apparatus of theological interpretation has grown up around it. Yet there are the bread and wine in their first simplicity, as when Jesus gave them to his disciples in the Upper Room.

Meanwhile, religions in history, like families in homes, accumulate in the course of time an inordinate amount of irrelevant stuff. Every religion tends to get overelaborated intellectually and overdecorated aesthetically, until the contrast between the simple life of some historic founder and the lengthening creeds and rituals of later times becomes a felt rebuke. Thus, there has been in contemporary Christianity a desire to get back of all our denominational differences to the Jesus of the Gospels.

This "genetic" method of studying the facts has been widely applied to all religions and there has been in recent years great interest in the beginnings of religion among the most primitive peoples. The method has been so generally employed that we cannot ignore it. It carries with it, however, certain dangers against which we should be on our guard. In particular there is no reason to suppose that the pattern of religion is so constant that every religion will run the same course, through the same stages, to the same end. You cannot, for example, sow as a seed in any society the magic rites practiced by the Trobriand Islanders, or the Zuni Indians, and watch first the blade, then the ear, mature as the thirteenth chapter of First Corinthians. The assumption that you can do so is responsible for the well-meant but mistaken hope that we now know so much about these matters that a committee of our best anthropologists and theologians are in a position to draft for us some comprehensive religion which shall embody the best elements of all religions in a single and final whole.

II

Having safeguarded the subject at this point we are now in position to go on to say that we can learn a good deal about religion in general by studying it in its simplest forms as they exist among primitive peoples, peoples either who lived long ago or who are now living in secluded pockets of our present world. As my former colleague, the late Professor George Foot Moore tells us,

It is now the prevailing opinion among anthropologists that religion in some form or other is universal . . . [Scholars have] nowhere discovered irreligious men. . . . The universality of religion warrants the inference that it has its origin in a common motive, and the identity of the elementary notions that everywhere go with it implies that they are man's natural response to his environment and experience.[2]

All primitive religions assume that unseen and occult powers in the world around impinge upon man and his affairs. These powers are believed to be locally resident in particular places and objects, or manifest in the more extraordinary happenings of nature. So, for example, when, in a letter to a friend, William James described his experience of the San Francisco

[2] George Foot Moore, *The Birth and Growth of Religion* (New York: Charles Scribner's Sons, 1923), pp. 1-3.

earthquake, an instinctive feeling that he was in the grip of some elemental power rose up from his racial subconsciousness, and he spoke as primitive man might have spoken in the clutch of a circumstance that was beyond his control:

The last thing Bakewell said to me, while I was leaving Cambridge, was "I hope they'll treat you to a little bit of earthquake while you're there." . . . Well, when I lay in bed at about half-past five that morning, wide awake, and the room began to sway, my first thought was, "Here's Bakewell's earthquake, after all"; and when it went crescendo and reached fortissimo in less than half a minute, and the room was shaken like a rat by a terrier, with the most vicious expression you can possibly imagine, it was to my mind absolutely an entity that had been waiting all this time holding back its activity, but at last saying, "Now, go it!" and it was impossible not to conceive it as animated by a will, so vicious was the temper displayed.[8]

The instinctive human response to such a situation is the old cry, "What must I do to be saved?" From that stark need something like the religious consciousness is born. Hence Professor Moore's simple statement, "If we seek a motive (i.e., for the birth of religion) universal, supreme, perpetual, it will be found in the impulse to self-preservation." This gen-

[8] *The Letters of William James* (Boston: The Atlantic Monthly Press, 1920), Vol. II, p. 248.

eric fact survives even though the self to be saved is soul rather than body.

One whole group of scholars in the field think of this self-preservation as best achieved in the terms of the identification of the individual with the solidarity of the tribe. The rugged individualist does not exist among primitive peoples, or if he exists he is suspected and outlawed as inimical to the integrity of the group. There is no "self-sufficing power of solitude" in such societies and we cannot read back the loneliness of the Hebrew prophet in Tekoa or of Jesus in the Garden into the more distant past. Men at first lived and hunted in packs, and the pack had to hold together.

Therefore, many of the most characteristic religious rites of primitive man are associated with those times and events by means of which the individual is formally initiated into membership in the tribe. It is true that unseen powers were often invoked in this connection, but they were invoked because the ordinary social devices did not seem adequate to cover all contingencies. We meet these religious rites most often in connection with birth, adolescence, marriage, hunting, planting, reaping, war, death, and burial. Even to this day, persons who otherwise are wholly indifferent to religion seem to feel more at ease if they are married in church, if their children are duly baptized, and if their dead are consigned to the grave by a minister rather than an undertaker. But whatever be true of modern man, it is clear that religion is most

constantly and characteristically met in primitive societies on those occasions when the tribe seeks to reassure itself as to its integrity and perpetuity. For such
a society the irreligious man is the maverick in the
herd, the stray, solitary individual who by accident or
by stubborn perversity remains unbranded by religious
rites and therefore uninitiated into the social whole.

To many scholars in the field this sociological interpretation of the facts yields the only truth and the
whole truth of religion. They hold that they are doing
the subject signal service in ridding it of the mistaken
idea that unseen and occult powers are in any way
involved. They would agree that the gods probably
had to be invoked for countless centuries to fill the
gaps in man's knowledge of nature; but as man's
knowledge of his universe becomes more accurate and
comprehensive the gods should be dismissed as no
longer necessary for the understanding and the conduct of life. Religion, they say, can be rightly inter-
preted only as we see in it man's resolute attempt to
close up his own human ranks in a compact and or-
derly manner. The pass key to the mysteries of religion
is therefore deposited with those who are skilled in the
psychological and social sciences. Anything that an
astronomer, for example, may say about religion is now
declared to be irrelevant, if not impertinent, because
the stars are not our "affair" religiously.

A second group of scholars, without denying the social aspects of religion, are more impressed by man's

stubborn belief that he is somehow or other involved with the powers that his cosmic environment discovers to him. They see primitive man moving cautiously about in "worlds not realized," where powers of incalculable energy have their local habitations. These powers are not at first thought of as being spiritual or moral in any modern sense of those words. The attitude of a savage toward the place with which the power is identified is precisely your attitude and mine when we come upon some pylon which carries electric cables and bears a sign saying, "Danger! High Tension Wires!" Here is something to be dealt with carefully. The initial reaction is that of salutary dread. Hence the prominence of the idea of fear in most primitive religions. Given the wild forces which man meets in nature—lightning, floods, hurricanes, earthquakes—one can only say that fear is a not unnatural reaction to the elements when they are unleashed.

A simple and altogether noble statement of this reaction of primitive man to the incalculable world by which he is environed may be found in some words of an old Eskimo to Knud Rasmussen:

We do not all understand the hidden things, but we believe the people who say they do. We believe our *angagok* (i.e. magicians), and we believe them because we do not want to expose ourselves to the danger of famine and starvation. We believe in order to make our lives and our food secure. If we did not believe our magicians, the animals we hunt would make themselves invisible to us; if we did not follow their advice we should fall ill and die. . . . We observe our old customs, in order to hold the world up, for the powers must not be offended. . . . We are afraid of the great evil. Men are so helpless.[4]

Religion, so construed, becomes therefore mainly a matter of learning how to relate oneself to these elemental and often sinister powers that are not oneself. The high-voltage cables must be hedged about with a set of barbed-wire safeguards. In the technical language of anthropology, "Objects, persons, times, places or actions charged with Power are called tabu. . . . Tabu is a sort of warning. . . . Power has been stored up and we must be on our guard. . . . Man's reaction to it should maintain the proper distance. . . . Tabu then is the avoidance of deed or word, springing from awe in the presence of Power." The phenomena of religion so construed tend, of course, to cross-breed with the concern of a society for its safety. Hunting, war, sex relations, involve words and acts which have to be marked with danger signs since in these critical matters one must step carefully. The indignation which swept over the Western world when the Germans released their first gas attack in the Great War might be said to be akin to the dread incurred by the breaking of a primitive tabu. Something elemental in the scheme of things had been violated.

[4] James Hastings, Ed., *Encyclopedia of Religion and Ethics* (New York: Charles Scribner's Sons, 1912), Vol. V, p. 394a.

It is only after the passage of time, the scholars go on to tell us, that these local habitations or manifestations of power are given names, the names of gods. The power was there before any name was named. There were *di certi* and *di incerti*, gods who had been identified and gods who had not yet been identified. Because you now know their names, you know what to do in relation to the former; you do not know what to do with respect to the latter, you only know that they cannot be ignored and you must be careful.

Primitive man's attitude toward these powers and gods was by no means restricted to the initial emotion of fear. If there was bad luck to follow wrong relations with the power, good luck might follow right relations. It was tricky business at the best, but there was always the chance that there might be a pot of gold at the end of the rainbow. Hence the eventual ascription of good and evil to the gods, and the beginnings of a belief in some kind of moral attributes of the gods, based on processes of trial and error. If the powers punished mistaken address, they seemed also to reward right address.

From this interpretation of the phenomena we infer that from the first, man has apparently believed himself unable to live a life safely divorced from his universe as a whole. Powers that are other and more than human constantly impinge upon him and his security is mainly conditioned by his mastery of the ways in which he should relate himself to them. Primitive man, perhaps better than most of his successors, knows that "it is a fearful thing to fall into the hands of the living God," even though he has his happier intimations of what it might be "to serve him without fear." But whether bringing fear or peace of mind the thought of the gods has been for man a "Hound of Heaven" that has never ceased to beset him

> With unhurrying chase,
> And unperturbed pace,
> Deliberate speed, majestic instancy.

This brief account of the two major schools of thought, as they are concerned with the crude beginnings of religion, must suffice. What I have said is sketchy in the extreme; I can only hope that it is not, in its main outlines, flagrantly mistaken. And if we are anywhere near the truth of the matter we seem to discover, present from the first, two theories as to religion: it has on the one hand a social reference; it has on the other hand a cosmic reference. In general those emphases and that distinction survive and reappear even in the most modern interpretations of religion. I have lingered thus long over the far-off primitive fact, because I think it anticipates the major religious issue of our own time; namely, whether religion is merely a social pattern, or whether it is in some way our deliberate attempt to relate ourselves to the universe as a whole.

III

Meanwhile, as you come on to the mature forms of religious experience, you are not left in doubt as to the hallmarks of the religious man. Whatever else he may be, he is not the solitary, unrelated man. He is a man who believes that he belongs to some thing or some one other than himself. He has a cause or a concern to which he has pledged himself, or a beloved to whom he has given himself. Religion has for centuries used the word "lost" about the irreligious man, and theology has been at great pains to try to understand the nature of that lostness. I once heard a teacher of the New Testament say that "a man is lost when he gets away from the place where he belongs or the person to whom he belongs and is in danger of not getting back." If you have been lost in a fog in some little boat at sea, or lost in the woods, you can feel the force of those simple words. All the bearings of your life are gone, there is nothing identifiable to which you can relate yourself. Irreligion is an experience like that, the conviction that you do not know where you are because you seem to have nowhere to belong.

Conversely, that to which in religion you belong, has to your mind certain qualities which make the relation the distinctive thing it is. This that you belong to is something greater than yourself in its mere dimensions. It will outlive you; its life is longer than your life. For example, it was not until after the Exile that the individual Jew thought of himself as standing in a direct relation to God. In the religion of earlier Israel that relation was made possible only through membership in the people of Israel. Hence the conviction that the days of man are numbered, but the days of the years of Israel are innumerable. Putting your numbered human days in the keeping of the unnumbered years of your people is, qualitatively, one of man's most constant ways of experiencing religion.

This to which you belong is also stronger than you are, and by communion with it or membership in it, you share its strength. When the writer to the Hebrews says of the heroes of the faith, "Out of weakness they were made strong," he is describing another of the ways in which we experience religion. So the modern hymn writer says of God,

> I look to Thee in every need,
>   And never look in vain;
> I feel Thy strong and tender love,
>   And all is well again:
> The tho't of Thee is mightier far
> Than sin and pain and sorrow are.

What is, perhaps, still more to the point for the purposes of a mature religion, that to which we belong is morally better than we are. The practice of the Black Mass, with its dedication of oneself to the Prince of Evil and the Powers of Darkness has never bulked large in religion. This perversion has always been an aberration and an exception to the rule. Men may actually have been better than the gods whom they worshiped, but they have usually believed that the situation was the other way around. It is one of the conditions for being a god that he shall be better than his worshipers. In the maturest religions this better moral quality assumes its final aspect as absolute righteousness and holiness. So another hymn writer says,

> Eternal Light, Eternal Light,
>   How pure the soul must be,
> That shrinks not, but with calm delight,
> When placed within Thy searching sight,
>   Can live and look on Thee.

Meanwhile, just by knowing that you belong to such a god you become better. As Professor Peabody once put it, "When a man honestly says, 'Our Father who art in heaven,' he rises to strength and self-respect."

Religion, then, is belonging to something or some one more enduring, stronger, and better than yourself. What you belong to, in those terms, is for the purposes of your life, your god. This experience carries with it the conviction that the good name and the cause of your god matter more to you than your own comfort, security, and worldly well-being. It comforts you to know that though you perish, some divine truth abides. It steadies you to believe that though you may fall in the heat of battle, you are on the right man's side and he must win the day. The soldier in the wars, the scientist in his laboratory, the surgeon operating on an infected tissue which may be as fatal to him as to his patient, the aviator fighting his way through a mountain storm because the mails must be carried—all these know in the terms of their own tasks the quality of the religious experience. Let us appeal to the words of one of the philosophers of the last generation, who tried to put the case as simply as possible:

Wherever a man is so carried beyond himself whether for any other being, or for a cause or for a nation, that his personal fate seems to him as nothing in comparison to the happiness or triumph of the other, there you have the universal basis and structure of religion. Power and perfection . . . are that to which in religion we have given our heart away.

And now we can see from what we are saved, and how. We are saved, if we must have a word, from isolation; we are saved by giving ourselves to something which we cannot help holding supreme.

Every man, we must hope and believe, has somewhere an allegiance that binds him, some disloyalty which he would rather die than commit. And if you know what this is, then you know where his religion lies. "Where your treasure is"—it is a true saying.[5]

[5] Bernard Bosanquet, *What Religion Is* (New York: The Macmillan Company, 1920), pp. 5, 6.

IV

Now all the distinctions between the world's religions have their origin in the differences between the things or causes or persons to which men think they belong. When Stephen Decatur said, "My country right or wrong," he was giving expression to an idea which qualitatively was religious. But when Edith Cavell said, "Patriotism is not enough," she was giving expression to a religion which was broader and more comprehensive. Stephen Decatur's god was a more limited god than Edith Cavell's God. One might say that this experience of belonging to some thing or some one other than oneself is like a pebble dropped into a still pool. Circles begin to spread from the point where it falls and go on spreading until they cover the whole pool. So it is with religions. Gods as we first meet them tend to be local and limited; their circle is a near and narrow one. But the circle tends forever to widen out until at last it is itself the boundary of the All, and the god whom it finally reaches is the one God of the whole universe, not one of the lesser gods defined by some earlier and narrower circle.

This widening of the circle from its center is particularly true of the ethical tendencies of a religion. Professor Franz Boas says:

The one outstanding fact is that every society has two

distinct ethical standards, the one for the in-group, the other for the out-group. . . .

The ethical behavior of man is based everywhere on these principles and may be considered as a further development of the herd instinct of higher animals. These animals hold together as one group, offering protection to one another and showing aggressive hostility to other groups which are potential rivals for food supply or are enemies of the species.

On the whole the tendency has been the enlargement of the group in which the ethical standards of the in-group are valid. The great ethical leaders of all times have expanded the group to embrace all humanity, because they saw that the primitive concept of specific differences between the in-group and the outsider is not valid.[6]

Theoretically most moderns would agree that if there is any god of the world, other than ourselves, he must be a universal God. Practically, most of us still tend to fall short of that goal, and if the truth be told, the gods by whom our lives are determined are too often lesser gods than that; they are the half-gods of whom Emerson wrote, who linger long until the whole gods come.

Thus, it has often been pointed out in the last few years that we shall misunderstand modern Germany and Russia, if we think of them as lands which are subject merely to radical changes of a political and eco-

[6] Clifton Fadiman, Ed., *I Believe* (New York: Simon and Schuster, 1939), pp. 22-23.

nomic nature. Nazism and Communism must be understood primarily in the terms of religion. They are movements built around ideas of race, blood, and class, which are receiving all the passionate devotion that men give to religion, and which in turn do for their devotees what religions have always professed to do. Therefore you cannot deal with these movements in terms of politics and economics. You will have to match them with a religion which is more true and more adequate. They are fanaticisms, but they are religious fanaticisms. Therein lies their power and therein lies also their danger. They are hot religions, hot with passionate emotion, and the rest of the world cannot hope to dispel them by lukewarm religions, even though those religions profess to believe in one God and Father of all humanity, rather than in the lesser gods of some race, or blood stock, or social class. One of the problems which a theoretically adequate religion always faces, when it becomes a platitude, is how to generate the devotion which men will always give to inadequate religions. How shall we make men of the modern world love and serve the cause of internationalism with the same zeal which for four hundred years has been given to the religions of nationalistic patriotism? Any honest person must realize that, while many of the gods whom the modern world is serving seem able to give their followers that singleness of mind and sense of power which every religion should impart, these gods fall short of that which an adequate idea of God must now require. From the standpoint of the total history of religion, these fanatical cults of state, race, and class are throwbacks to a more primitive order of things, which by this twentieth century we might have hoped to have outgrown.

Meanwhile the prevalence of such religions raises afresh the problem already sighted in our brief account of beginnings; whether religion is primarily a matter of one's social reference and adjustments, or whether before all else it involves conscious relationship to a God who is apart from and more than our human selves. The kind of religion you profess and practice will depend upon your choice of one or the other of these alternatives, or if not upon a choice, then upon an emphasis.

In a famous sentence in the *Apologia* Cardinal Newman said that his mind rested "in the thought of two and two only luminously self-evident beings, myself and my Creator." Here is the cosmic reference alone, in apparent neglect of any social consciousness. Few Christians would be content to leave the matter there, unsupplemented and unverified by an awareness of their fellow men. In his swift and discriminating reduction of "all the law and the prophets" to two short sentences, Jesus linked love of the neighbor with love of God. Christianity has often suggested that the only certain proof we give of our love of the God whom we have not seen is love of our brother whom we have seen. Ideally the sociological and cosmic references, so far from being mutually exclusive, ought to supplement and confirm one another. But practically, as is the case with all these radical antitheses, each of us inclines in the conduct of life toward the one or the other.

In modern America, particularly so much of it as represents the more liberal Protestant tradition, it has been the social aspects of religion which have attracted us most and apparently have satisfied us best. We are a practical people; we understand good works better than we understand prayer. Given the diversity of our racial and cultural origins, the problem of organizing neighborliness in the name of religion has been sufficiently complex and imperative to monopolize our attention. For, being neighbors in America calls for something more than a natural fellow feeling for your own particular kind. To the initial statement of the problem presented by the diversities of race and tradition in America, the intense industrialization of life has added its own more recent problems. If we have had to make doorways through the vertical partitions that separate us racially and culturally, we have also had to build stairways to provide means of communication between the various social levels of the community. This opening up and freeing of our "house of God," so that it shall not remain a series of cells in a prison block, where single groups live in solitary confinement—"rotting away unheeded and alone in the isolated dungeon of their self-consciousness," as

Royce has it—has claimed and absorbed most of our religious energies. The American temperament being what it is, practical and activistic, and the American problem being what it has been up to date, it would be strange if the emphasis had been placed elsewhere.

But since all this is a matter of the very air we breathe and a thing of mental second nature rather than of conscious choice, we do not realize how far the pendulum has swung away from awareness of some God-other-than-ourselves, and toward a merely human interpretation of religion. This was, I think, one of the discoveries which most American delegates to the Oxford and Edinburgh Conferences made, when they saw themselves, not merely as others see them, but as they indubitably are. Our confidence in the psychological and sociological methods of interpreting religion, which are so familiar to Americans and so characteristic of us, is looked at askance by many Christians in the Old World who, rightly or wrongly, incline in the other direction.

Let it be said at once that we repudiate in theory, and are still struggling to frustrate in fact, any social interpretation of religion which stops short of the race in its entirety. The best exponents of religion, socially construed, would hold that no religion can square with what we now know religion ought to be, if it does not propose to make a man a conscious and responsible member of humanity as a whole. This humanity must include—as Edmund Burke has it—"not only those who are living, but those who are living, those who are dead, and those who are to be born."[7] If its breadth should be as wide as all men now living in this generation, its length should link all human generations in a single experience and endeavor. Walt Whitman has said this, nobly, in his lines on "Crossing Brooklyn Ferry":

Flood-tide below me! I see you face to face!
Clouds of the west—sun there half an hour high—I see you also face to face.

Crowds of men and women attired in the usual costumes, how curious you are to me!

[7] For the sake of those who may not know the reference, I am minded to insert here the whole passage. It comes from Burke's *Reflections on the Revolution in France*. Burke is commenting upon the "social contract" theory of the State, and is saying that any adequate conception of the State requires time and tradition, as well as agreement among contemporaries. What he says of the State holds true of the Church, as a historical institution, and is a needed corrective for too short-range theories of churches organized on the congregational polity.

"Society is indeed a contract. Subordinate contracts for objects of mere occasional interest may be dissolved at pleasure—but the state ought not to be considered as nothing better than a partnership agreement in a trade of pepper and coffee, callico or tobacco, or some other such low concern, to be taken up for a little temporary interest, and to be dissolved by the fancy of the partners. It is to be looked on with reverence; because it is not a partnership in things subservient only to the gross animal existence of a temporary and perishable nature. It is a partnership in all science; a partnership in all art; a partnership in every virtue, and perfection. As the ends of such a partnership cannot be obtained in many generations, it becomes a partnership not only between those who are living, but between those who are living, those who are dead, and those who are to be born. Each contract of each particular state is but a clause in the great primeval contract of eternal society, linking the lower and higher natures, connecting the visible and invisible world."

On the ferry-boats the hundreds and thousands that cross,
    returning home are more curious to me than you sup-
    pose.

And you that shall cross from shore to shore years hence
    are more to me, more in my meditation, than you might
    suppose. . . .

It avails not, time nor place—distance avails not,
I am with you, you men and women of a generation, or
    ever so many generations hence. . . .

What is the count of the scores or hundreds of years
    between us? . . .

Closer yet I approach you,
What thought you have of me now, I had as much of
    you. . . .

We understand then do we not?

Such is the social gospel, when it is lifted above the
dusty level of political and economic readjustments to
its height and length and breadth as the experience
of belonging to a "Beloved Community of Memory
and Hope." In its own terms this is essentially a mystical interpretation of man's life as a member of the
race, and is a profoundly moving and satisfying intimation of religion.

   To such a religion in its ideal dimensions we now
give the name of "humanism." Humanism is religion
construed as the sum of a man's right relations to all
his fellow men, shorn of the idea that any Cod, in the

traditional meaning of that word, is the premise for that relation or is involved in it as a third partner. The humanist is not, of course, necessarily an atheist; that is, he does not deny that there may be a supernatural divine being. He is merely agnostic; he says that he does not know. In any case he says that there is no longer any occasion for using the old-fashioned ideas of God, since he holds that a more accurate knowledge of nature and history now makes it unnecessary to invoke a god, either to understand their processes or to control them. We do these things for ourselves now-a-days in the intelligible and manageable terms of our own human skills.

This interpretation of religion is accepted today by a much larger number of men and women than we might suppose. Canon Barry of Westminster has gone so far as to say that humanism is today the working religion of fifty per cent of the intelligent persons in the modern world. The religion of humanism, which is in part the product of our constantly increasing understanding of natural processes, and in still greater part the product of a conscience that is forever becoming more impatient with the world's evils, is not in the main organized in churches. It has been called "The Religion of All Good Men." Among the rank and file of professional people—teachers, scholars, doctors, lawyers, artists—and more conscientious men in business and public life, the religion of humanism exists as a widespread and powerful force. To its prevalence we owe the high ethical standards of the professions when they are at their best, and that sense of duty to our fellow men which is woven as a constant bright thread across the darker warp of life.

Not only is this unorganized, unecclesiastical religion powerfully operative among men today, for all practical purposes it has become the interpretation of religion stressed by churches which have grown up within liberal democratic societies. The old ideas of sovereignty and serfdom which furnished the metaphors for the elder doctrines of God and man have passed away out of our common life. We have to make a deliberate act of imagination to understand what is meant by God, a king and sovereign. There is no ground left in our life for those metaphors. The fact is that most moderns suspect appeals to the supernatural of being—in the language of the new psychology—escape mechanisms made use of by those who are not strong enough to stand up to life—of being, in Gilbert Murray's famous phrase about the last stage of Greek religion, the sign of "a failure of nerve." We could not respect ourselves if we feared that our religion was another such failure of nerve. These and many other forces have conspired to make the average American Christian a person for whom his religion, whatever he may say in church on Sunday, is a six-day of the week attempt to get the best conscience of the age socially organized and implemented. For countless of our contemporaries this is more than enough to comprise a satisfying religion; for many of them it is the whole truth and the only truth of religion. All else has been proved outworn and irrelevant.

v

Let us turn in conclusion to the other interpretation of religion; that it is before all else a matter of man's relation to God. We shall have more to add to this subject when we come to our final chapter. Meanwhile I can only say that to my own mind there is, for religion, no other single religious issue as important as that between humanism and theism.

You will remember the dramatic passage at the beginning of *Thus Spake Zarathustra*:

When Zarathustra went down the mountain alone, he entered the forest and there suddenly stood before him an old man who had left his holy cot to seek roots.

"And what doth the saint in the forest?" asked Zarathustra. The saint answered: "I make hymns and sing them; and in making hymns I laugh and weep and mumble; thus do I praise God. But what dost thou bring us as a gift?"

When Zarathustra heard these words, he bowed to the saint and said: "What should I have to give thee: Let me rather hurry hence lest I take aught away from thee!"

When Zarathustra was alone, however, he said to his heart: "Could it be possible! The old saint in the forest hath not yet heard of it, that *God is dead!*"

When he has the courage of his convictions, this is what the humanist says. For the purposes of religion *God is dead*. But is he? That is the question. One is reminded of the story told of Robert Louis Stevenson: while he was staying at Saranac on his trip across America, news came to the snowbound cabin where he and his companions were lodged that Matthew Arnold had died. No one said anything: plainly the first word belonged to Stevenson, who paced up and down before the fire for a while and finally looked up and said, "He won't like God!" The humanist must face that possibility! As Browning puts it, "just when we're safest," having put all such possibilities away as outworn superstitions, we are again confronted by "the grand Perhaps."

So, a modern writer, using for the moment untheological language, has given us a brief, stirring essay which he calls "My Neighbor the Universe." Again, this is the problem. Is the universe your neighbor, or is it an utter stranger and alien to you? A friend once said to Frederick W. H. Myers, "If you could ask the Sphinx one question, and one only, what would that question be?" Myers replied, "If I could ask one question and one only, and hope for an answer, I think the question would be this, 'Is the universe friendly?'" That is the first and last of all questions about religion. Is there some kind of correspondence and commerce between man and his world as a whole, between himself and God? Or is there no such correspondence, and is the boundary line between man's affairs and the "passionless impersonality of the unknown and the unknowable" closed to all travel and spiritual commerce?

I am quite willing to concede that such problems are beyond our power to solve to our final satisfaction. When faith has done its best there will remain, for knowledge, vast margins of ignorance and of uncertainty. I can wholly share Whittier's plight;

> The same old baffling questions! O my friend,
> I cannot answer them. In vain I send
> My soul into the dark, where never burn
> The lamps of science, nor the natural light
> Of Reason's sun and stars.

But I am concerned that we should not close the doors too soon and too easily against the possibility of a high neighborliness with the universe, as well as with the man in the next street or the next country. Because the possibility of such neighborliness is beyond scientific proof, let alone imagination, we tend to shut our modern minds to the God who hides himself in Infinite Mystery.

But it is not as though the cult of humanism had so proved its case up to the hilt that it is now possible to believe easily in a sociological religion, and impossible to believe in a cosmic religion. If theism has been tried and found wanting, humanism has not yet finally vin-

dicated itself. Even in those circles which still have
enough moral idealism to equate humanism with
membership in the race in its entirety, the voice of
the people gives an uncertain sound. The nineteenth
and early twentieth centuries have been, in Europe
and America, the great humanistic age of the Christian era. If the believer in God is today hard put to
it to find his God in the welter of world wars which
seem now to have become epidemic, the humanist is
not in much better case. One modern interpreter of humanism has had the candor to say, "The question is no
longer whether we can believe in God, but how and
in what way we can continue to believe in man." The
faith of the humanist, with his belief in man, seems to
me in the face of present facts, as naïve and as hard to
hold as that faith in God which he repudiates. In
short Zarathustra does not solve our religious problem by his dogmatic statement that *God is dead.*
Nietzsche died in a madhouse, and he must turn un-
easily in his grave when he dreams of the present
doings of his Superman.

For, see what it comes down to, if we cannot believe
that there is some deep and enduring correspondence
between man and his universe—want of this faith
means that natural forces which themselves know
nothing of such things have cast up out of the slime
at the sea edge a creature who is capable of infinite
longings, who mistakenly feels himself made for immortality, who can know tempests in the mind that

make all else seem calm, and who dies knowing that his world, which knows not what it is doing, slays him. (These are familiar phrases from the Bible, from Shakespeare, from Pascal.) It means that of all the ironies and tragedies which ingenuity might conceive, none could be greater than this, that there will come a time on this planet when not a wrack of all that man has been and known and felt shall remain. The amazing accident that was humanity will have passed utterly away. The race and its whole history is already in the hands of a receiver. Though the universe may not foreclose on us for millions of years, there is no possibility that we can ever work off the mortgage or escape from the receivership. We shall go on doing our decent human business from generation to generation, perhaps declaring now and then some small cash dividend. But redeeming the principal is beyond our powers, and at the last human life will end as "a tale told by an idiot, full of sound and fury, signifying nothing." We may take comfort from thinking that all this is so remote that it does not concern us and we need not worry. But to thoughtful persons such considerations make a subtle difference, emotionally perhaps, rather than morally. A certain sadness and awareness of waning vitality attend the conviction that all our human concerns are doomed to end as dust blown between the worlds by winds which even now can be felt, as Kipling has it, cutting us to the bone.

It is the prudent reluctance of the humanist to admit the final stages of his logic that enables him to win short-term converts to his creed. He wisely refrains from drawing in public the conclusions to which his premises commit him. He may be right. We must always face that possibility. If so, we must align ourselves with Bertrand Russell and hereafter build our soul's citadel upon "the firm foundation of unyielding despair."

In deciding whether you wish any religion at all, and if so what kind of a religion you wish and where your emphasis shall fall, you ought to take these longer considerations into account. The somber prospect which an unequivocal humanism holds out to us is that of an overcast afternoon, graying into the darkness of a night from which there shall be for humanity no awakening. Confronted with this possibility we may shrink from it, and by wishful thinking build for ourselves a city of refuge from "dreadful night." The possibility of just such a failure of nerve and of willful self-deception must be reckoned with.

But in spite of the plausibility of humanism, I can only say that merely as a matter of probability, it seems to me more likely that man has some eternal correspondence and commerce with his universe, than that he is an amazing biological accident destined to become an ironic tragedy in a universe which is unconscious of him and indifferent to him. The astronomer tells us that at the very remotest boundaries of his galaxies the elements which make up the stars are the elements we know here; iron is iron whether here or there. We may not press the analogy, but neither can we ignore it.

My own faith is that religion is primarily man's thoughtful relation to some kindred process in the totality of things, and that his world of human relations is a corollary and consequence of that prior fact. If I were to put the grounds for the sociological interpretation of religion in traditional terms I should say that all we are brethren, because one is our Father, and that in want of the latter belief, faith in ourselves and our brother is harder to realize rather than easier. As for my major emphasis, that religion is before all else a matter of our relation to God, I have long turned to Saint Augustine for a classic statement of that faith:

O God, Thou hast made us for Thyself and our hearts are restless until they find rest in Thee. . . .

The "social" corollary follows, again in Augustine's words:

Blessed is he who loves Thee, and his friend in Thee, and his enemy for Thee. For he alone loses no one dear to him, to whom all are dear in Him who never can be lost.

Chapter II

FAITH

IN A FAMOUS LETTER TO CHARLES KINGSLEY, THOMAS HUXLEY ONCE SAID, "THE LONGER I LIVE, THE MORE obvious it is to me that the most sacred act of a man's life is to say and to feel, 'I believe such and such to be true.' All the greatest rewards and all the heaviest penalties of existence cling about that act."

Religion is charged with the custody of life's sacred things, and if "to believe" is a sacred act, then faith is necessary to religion. Such, indeed, is the common conviction, and most of us would agree not merely that religion presupposes faith, but that the attitude and exercise of faith are the distinguishing characteristics of religion.

Within the circle of religion itself the idea antithetical to faith is that of doubt. But when we contrast religion with the rest of our interests the antithesis to faith is knowledge. I should like to linger for a little over this latter antithesis, because a great many persons today seem to take it for granted that knowing things is an easy act while believing is hard. One of the handicaps under which religion labors today is the popular notion that religion is merely a matter of muddying the otherwise clear stream of experience, of "kicking up a dust and then complaining that we cannot see."

I

In the division of our intellectual enterprises the areas of the unknown, if they are to be possessed at all, must be possessed by faith and are assigned to religion; the areas which have been or presumably can be possessed by knowledge are assigned to science. Many persons in both camps feel therefore that there is no conflict between science and religion simply because, when each is properly employed with its own affairs, the two will never come into collision. They meet at a boundary line which at any given moment is more or less well defined, but their territories do not overlap. There is, I think, much to be said for this simple initial solution of the vexed problem of the interrelation of science and religion. Faith must concede to knowledge its assured conquests. Knowledge cannot deny to faith its right to adventure into the unknown. This is not the whole truth of the situation; it is a relevant half-truth.

But the process of knowing things and the nature of the knowledge achieved are not apparently as simple as we sometimes seem to imply. Most colleges offer, through their philosophy departments, a course in "epistemology"—dealing with the theory of the method and grounds of knowledge. If you ever come to the time when you think that knowing things is a plain and easy matter I suggest that you take this course in epistemology. It is not a snap course, and unless you put your brains to it the chances are that you may flunk altogether. And if you succeed in passing its final examination you will come away a soberer and a humbler knower.

The truth is that in the back of the minds of many of the most thoughtful men down the centuries there has been a gnawing doubt as to whether we really know anything. It is one of the paradoxes of life that the world's intellectually keenest minds have very often turned from a naïve confidence in knowledge to the praise of ignorance. This paradox has passed into the wisdom of the race. "And I gave my heart," says the author of *Ecclesiastes*, "to seek and search out by wisdom concerning all things that are done under Heaven: this sore travail hath God given the sons of men to be exercised therewith. Yea, my heart had great experience of wisdom and knowledge. I perceived that this also is vexation of spirit. For in much wisdom is much grief; and he that increaseth knowledge increaseth sorrow." The happiest life, says a Latin proverb, is to know nothing, *nihil scire est vita jucundissima.* "He alone is wise," runs another maxim, "who knows that he knows nothing." All this was two thousand or twenty-five hundred years ago, but the strain persists down to our own day. Henry Adams tells us that when he came back to Harvard as a teacher of history he "was crushed by his own ignorance, and jostled by a crowd of men who seemed to him ignorant that there was a thing called ignorance." The familiar story of his *Education*—one of the most brilliant autobiographies of our time—ends, in its author's own words in *The Abyss of Ignorance.* "Never," he writes of himself in the third person, "had the proportions of ignorance looked so appalling. He seemed to know nothing, and the worst depth consisted in the assurance, incredible as it seemed, that no one knew more." There is no need to labor the point. Let it suffice to point out in passing that many thoughtful men do not find the process of knowing a simple one or the resulting knowledge self-vindicating.

II

Having said so much by way of warning I shall assume, for the further purposes of this lecture, that we agree that knowledge does exist, and that it is probably best exemplified in the findings of science. All sciences begin with accurate observation of facts and processes. Ideally a science demands a laboratory where the supply of material is adequate and where processes may be repeated until certain recurring and constant uniformities are identified. These observed uniformities are then codified as the laws of nature and history. The goal at which science aims is prediction, the ability to tell how things will behave in the future. By such

means the scientist gives us the split second at which
the next total eclipse of the sun will begin, and can
mark across the map of continents and seas the dark
band of its totality. The laboratory need not be a room
in a building; it may as well be the starry heavens, or
a ward in a hospital, or a teeming city full of people.
In the world of given facts and observable processes
there are no subjects that are not the proper concern
of science.

Scientists themselves would be the first to admit
that they achieve varying degrees of certainty, according to their fields. It is said that strictly speaking
there is only one exact science—mathematics. But a
science like physics aspires to exactness and often ap-
proximates to it. When you come to the disciplines
which deal with man, such as psychology and sociology, mathematical precision becomes more difficult to
attain, because the number of imponderables in the
situation is so greatly increased. Practitioners in a field
like history are divided among themselves as to whether
their concern is not as much an art as a science. But
whatever the degrees of uncertainty in the scale of the
sciences, they all look with single eye to the ideal of
certitude and tend steadily in that direction. One can
only say that, given the tremendous achievements of
the sciences in the last century or so, its advocates have
every reason to have confidence in their method and
loyalty to their ideal. Vast areas, which for centuries
had been dark continents of ignorance, have been con-

quered and colonized by knowledge. Dread of the unknown has been banished from one phase after another of our experience, and we move about our world today with a confidence, almost a nonchalance, which would have seemed to our predecessors little short of suicidal folly.

Now one of the reasons, in some ways perhaps the most considerable single reason, for the decay of religion in the modern world is precisely the signal success of the sciences in extending so widely the area of man's knowledge. Religion is prompted in no small part by man's capacity for wonder and his tendency to worship. What Coleridge says of philosophy can be just as well said of religion. It "begins in wonder and ends in wonder; and the interspace is filled with admiration." Religion is also prompted by man's desire to understand his world, himself and his experience. Now, on either count, whether of wonder or of understanding, science has pre-empted many of the moods and concerns which previously men have identified with religion. The visitor to a World's Fair goes with dropping jaw and goggling eyes from one marvel to another. What need has he of more wonders than these to satisfy his capacity for admiration carried almost to the point of worship. At least that was the way Henry Adams felt when he looked at the "Dynamo," at the Chicago World's Fair in 1893. He was prepared to say his prayers to it, so fully did it incarnate in modern terms the presence of a "power." Indeed, in a memorable poem, he did say that prayer. And when it comes to understanding things, science has discovered so many near-at-hand causes for particular facts and events, that the first and final causes of all things are put beyond the margin of the mind's present concern. Men once thought that God sent the hurricane as a direct sign of his anger and vehicle of his vengeance. They now know that hurricanes are created by varying temperatures of sea and land surfaces, by sharp contrasts between the states of upper and lower airs, and with that knowledge they are content, since the weather man can now predict hurricanes in time for us to get ready for them. God as a direct author of happenings in nature and history is pushed off into the distance.

It is said that a certain Spanish cardinal in the thirteenth century was the last man who could know everything that was known in his day. After him the human mind suffered fission, and it took first two men, then four, and eight, to know what was known, until who shall say today how many minds would be required to compass the width and breadth of the reliable knowledge of our twentieth century? I once estimated that a student would have to spend a hundred and four years in Harvard to take the general courses announced in the catalogue, and even then he would only have scratched the surface of what is now known. With such an opportunity at his very door, why should a man send his mind still farther afield? Here is enough to occupy him for his three score years and ten, and even then leave the task unfinished. It was in this spirit that Robert Browning put back into the lips of Paracelsus in the days of the Renascence the faith professed by the pure sciences of our day with their passion to know, and their advance assurance of accessible knowledge:

> How comes it . . .
> . . . that when, quailing at the mighty range
> Of secret truths which yearn for birth, I haste
> Undazzled to contemplate some one truth,
> Its bearings and effects alone—at once
> What was a speck expands into a star,
> Asking a life to pass exploring thus,
> Till I near craze.

Furthermore, unless we are to regard knowledge as being by its very nature excluded from the concerns of religion, there is no reason why we should not rejoice at this vast extension of modern knowledge. It is, alas, still hard for many pious persons to realize that whenever we have found a new truth, whatever its content, and however that truth may conflict with what religion had once believed, we have come so much nearer reality, nearer to that God who is the God of all truth. College students, at least, ought not to be afraid of anything that knowledge can do to religion; they ought, on the contrary, to rejoice in what it does for religion. They should be heartened by those familiar words about the goal of religion. "Now we see through a glass darkly . . . now I know in part, but then shall I know even as also I am known." It is said in the Bible that there will be no church in heaven. We are apparently to infer that by the time heaven has come to pass churches, as institutions serving the Kingdom of God, will have done their work and will thereafter be superfluous. So one might dare to say that in heaven there will be no place or need for faith as our way of relating ourselves to the unknown, because all will be known at last and faith will have been fulfilled in knowledge. Faith seems, therefore, even here and now to be an act forever in process of passing over into knowledge. Therefore the ideal which science sets before itself of full and final knowledge cannot be one from which religion turns away, since it is the nature and destiny of faith to end in knowledge.

Now there are a great many scientists who are quite willing to admit that there well may be some truth in religion—at least they do not deny the possibility. But they plead their preoccupation with more pressing concerns nearer at hand. Their mood is that of the famous line from *Candide*—"*Il faut cultiver notre jardin.*" We've enough work to do tidying up our own front yard. Their attitude has many counterparts, is wholly intelligible, and up to a point defensible. The problem of world peace might be cited as a parallel, a problem which is hopelessly intricate in its statement and far beyond the mental power of the plain man to understand; why should he not therefore concern himself with situations he can grasp and manage, his home and his business? The difficulty is, of course, that try as he may to keep his home and his business tidy, they are getting terribly untidied year after year by the environing world situation. So, we might say, any man, in getting some decent understanding of chemistry or sociology, has enough to occupy his mind for a lifetime. The universe is a vast incomprehensible affair. Why tackle its infinities? But, the trouble is that the tidied-up front yards of the separate sciences are constantly getting untidied by goings-on in neighboring yards and even more by changes in the wider world round about.

The idea of "agnosticism," by which the cult of one's own tidied-up front yard may be defended, is open to abuse as well as to proper use. It is true, as science tells us, that most of the concerns of religion lie in areas where exact knowledge is impossible: it is not true that these areas do not impinge upon us and that we can succeed in permanently shutting them out of our reckoning. Job came to the moment, in his attempt to understand his experience, when he deliberately fell back upon agnosticism. "Once have I spoken; but I will not answer: yea, twice; but I will proceed no further." The story does not stop there. It goes right on: "Then answered the Lord unto Job out of the whirlwind, and said, Gird up thy loins now like a man: I will

demand of thee, and declare thou unto me." Agnosticism becomes an indefensible attitude toward life
when it sinks to the level of studied indifference. It
is not our inability to know that is at fault; it is the premature peace we are content to make with our ignorance. Being human is facing life's first and last
problems, to many of which only the adventurous answers of faith can be given. And to fail to venture those
answers is to deny one's human nature and to shirk
one's human duty. Why are we here? What is the
good life? How shall we find true happiness? What
will it all come to in the end? Science does not know
the answer to any one of these questions, yet they are
the most important questions that life puts to us, and
we cannot either properly or safely evade them. To
take refuge in one's own front yard and never to look
over the fence one builds about that yard is, after all,
merely one form of asceticism; an asceticism addressed
to the mind rather than the body, but none the less
ascetic on that account.

This well-known habit of modern science, of dis-
claiming responsibility for life as a whole and restricting itself to limited truths of a highly specialized type,
is in no small part chargeable for the mounting unease
with which men as a whole are today viewing the
sciences. Fifty years ago, when the scientific movement
was in the first full flush of its enthusiasms, countless
persons believed that it should be science which should
deliver man from those errors and ills that had taken

toll of him for centuries. Alas, this trust has not been redeemed. The state of the Western world at the present moment is not such as to reassure men as to the validity and finality of the messianic mission of modern science. A distinguished historian of science told me not long since that, during a sabbatical year in Europe, he had visited many of the most famous continental scientists and that there was observable everywhere among them a note of pessimism as to what science has actually achieved and perhaps can achieve in making a world at peace. It has failed to redeem its brave pledges of the last century, and its findings have far too often been turned to evil rather than good account. In short our success with specialized technical skills has not succeeded in consolidating our world as a whole, or helping us understand life as a whole. We have, it is true, pushed the borders of our knowledge much farther out than ever before into the domain of old ignorance, but as we extend these borders the horizons recede, and beyond all that we now know there still lies a realm of mystery, with its inscrutable riddles.

III

Now in the division of functions and labors we may say with entire propriety that it is the office of faith to take up the task of trying to relate ourselves to our world at the point where scientific knowledge is compelled to lay it down. This is admittedly a bold task, perhaps an impossible task. But it is not an unnatural task, nor an indefensible one. The Bible says that Abraham was the father of the faithful. The distinguishing mark of his life and character was, according to the old story, the fact that he went out from a world which was known into a world that was unknown. The New Testament says of him that "he went out, not knowing whither he went."

Something of that quality will always attach to the act of believing, and to the nature of religious faith. There have been men in Christian history, and movements, who strove to emphasize the unreasonable element in faith. Very early in the history of the church we meet the statements, "I believe because it is absurd —I believe because it is impossible." Late in his life, when he had lost his intellectual courage, Martin Luther said that reason is an ugly devil's bride, and that it is the business of faith to strangle reason and slay her. This tendency to do violence to one's reason is always reappearing in Christian history and is difficult to understand. Apparently it comes sometimes from that "failure of nerve" which Gilbert Murray discusses. Men seem to feel that they have been intellectually presumptuous and overbold. In other instances you get this strain among men who are, so to speak, overintellectual—that is, men who have developed their minds at the expense of their emotions and their wills. In still other instances anti-intellectualism is, as I have already suggested, a cropping out in the terms of the mind of the particular forms of religious perversion which we meet in extreme asceticism, with its insistence that a man give himself pain and do himself hurt. There are in religion intellectual ascetics who scourge their minds as other fanatics have scourged their bodies. However these things may be, we are witnessing at the moment, in various religious quarters, a cropping up of this deliberate cult of irrationality in the name of faith. The reappearance of these tendencies in our own time is not inexplicable; it is a by-product of the disappointments, the weariness, the disillusionment of our generation—the feeling that a century and a half of science and "sweet reasonableness" and brutal wars have got us nowhere.

But I would point out that all such movements are incidental to the main course of the history of Christian thought, not its essence. The Christian religion has always been, technically, one of the world's learned religions. It has its sacred book; it has its uninterrupted succession of interpreters of that book. It has its complex systems of Christian thought, as intricate and majestic as its cathedrals. More thinking has been spent on the Christian religion in the last two thousand years than on any other single concern of the Western world. Even if the results of that thought are incomplete and inconclusive, few of us would say that this thinking has been unwarranted and useless. When Saint Paul speaks of "our reasonable service" to God, he is running true to Christian form. Christianity has always had a sobriety of mind, and at its best has never been a matter of madness or daydreaming, but rather has cherished the conviction that its beliefs are a kind of sanctified common sense. Faith, then, is the name which we give to our meditative attitude toward the mysteries by which we are surrounded, mysteries which are still hidden from us, but from which we cannot, whether we would or no, escape.

Following up the clue given him by the ancient and classical story of Abraham going out he knew not where, into an undiscovered country, the writer of the Epistle to the Hebrews suggests that faith is giving substance to things hoped for. This general conception of religious faith as being the endeavor to vindicate an hypothesis is one which is perfectly intelligible to science, and which of itself ought to present no difficulties to the scientific mind. Science always approaches facts not yet understood with some advance theory as to what they are and how they work. It tries out its hypotheses to see whether the facts bear them out. It sometimes fails, often fails, but again and again it succeeds. The most daring work in science is always done by persons who bring such hypotheses to the facts. The theory-in-advance is certainly not knowledge, you can only say that it is more akin to faith. So in religion the believer is not taking farewell of his reason, or even of the sober scientific processes of his mind. He is, rather, extending a method in which he has learned to have confidence into areas where as yet anything like certain verification is not to be had soon or easily.

Religion has allowed itself in these recent years to be thrown far too much upon the defensive, as being an intellectual and moral adventure in excess of anything that reason can countenance, as being wishful thinking, as being an escape mechanism for defeated souls who are not strong enough to stand up against the hard facts of a stern world. Religion has tended to forget what any good soldier knows that the best defense is a strong offense.

Certainly we have no scientifically verifiable proof of the existence of God, of the superiority in the scheme of the universe of good over evil or even of any awareness of such a distinction, of the possibility or probability of any life beyond this present life that we now live. In the scientific sense of the term you cannot know these things, you can only believe them. You can assume in advance that they are realities and that on the whole such facts as you do know are more intelligible on this basis than on any other. You have a perfect right to conclude that in spite of many facts pointing in other directions, there are enough facts pointing in this direction to warrant your making the venture.

When Columbus set out to sail westward from Europe he did not do so in a purely agnostic frame of mind. He had a theory that there was land to the west.

He thought, of course, that the Indies could be
reached by going in that direction. His reasons for believing that there was something there in the west
were not inconsiderable. At various times on the coast
of Europe intimations of such a world had been
washed ashore; the body of a dark man with a flat face
unlike that of any European, a strangely carved piece
of wood which had no parallel in the Old World, seeds
borne by the wind which yielded tropical plants not
known in Spain and Portugal. He put these hints together and embarked on a risky adventure, but no one
can say that it was an unreasonable voyage, although
it went beyond any knowledge that men then had.

So it is, let us say, with the idea of God and with
faith in God. No man hath seen God at any time.
But theology has said that the attributes of God, his
spiritual tempers and characteristics, find expression
in this world in facts and processes which are observable. Two groups of men first achieved what we might
call the idea of one God and Father of us all, the
Hebrew prophets and the Greek philosophers. The
prophets got their first glimpses of such a God in the
terms of righteousness. The Greeks got this idea from
their feeling for beauty, and Plato rose from the sight
of beautiful things in an ascending scale, to the idea of
Universal Beauty reigning in the universe. A friend of
mine told me of seeing the other day some of the incredibly rapid motion pictures which are now being
taken at the Massachusetts Institute of Technology—

perhaps you have seen the photograph of a golf swing, the club caught at a hundred points in its arc. My friend had seen in those pictures the fluttering of the wings of a humming bird, which the human eye never sees. He had seen a drop of milk falling into a saucer of milk, showing the circular crown formed by the process, a perfect coronet having its rim raised above the level of the liquid in the dish, with little prongs rising regularly around the rim, and each prong tipped with a perfect pearl—a thing incredibly beautiful. And he said, "How can one doubt that all these little formal happenings in the world of nature, each so perfect and lovely, are so many hints as to the nature of the whole of things?" It was an experience of this sort that led an ancient writer to say, "The first author of beauty hath created them." I must say that as life goes on, the wanton and prodigal beauty of nature as seen in homely and familiar things impresses me more and more. Are these bits of beauty merely so many random accidents or acts of deliberate deception on the part of a universe that is itself indifferent to beauty, if not ugly at heart? I can only say that such a theory seems to me less likely, and to call for a more perverse faith, than the simple inference that "the author of beauty hath created them."

Faith, then, so construed, is a spiritual adventure in attempted vindication of its hypotheses; God, truth, goodness, beauty, immortality. Wordsworth says of such adventurers that they go "voyaging through strange seas of thought, alone," and that is quite true. But it is from just such voyages of thought into unknown seas that all of man's knowledge has come thus far. The man who believes has as many initial reasons for believing as has the doubter for his doubts, and the burden of proof is just as much on the man who denies as on the man who affirms.

IV

There is another aspect of faith to which I turn in conclusion, in the attempt to distinguish it from the knowledge we get from the sciences, and, therefore, to define its distinctive task.

It is not the business of science to pass moral judgments, to say of its subjects that they reveal a better and a worse. That is, science has nothing to do with what we call the world of values. When it begins to pass what are known as "value-judgments" it is, given its own premises, out of bounds. For example, Havelock Ellis wrote five volumes on *The Psychology of Sex*. He describes at length, not merely all the normal emotions which attend the direct and forthright expressions of sex, he goes also into the painful details of every one of the known abuses and perversions which attend this elemental fact. But never once in all his thousands of pages does he venture to say, "This conduct is right, and that conduct is wrong; this act is good and that act is bad." He does, it is true, describe the consequences to body and mind of various courses of action, but he leaves the matter there. In short, he writes as psychologist, a scientist pure and simple; he does not profess to be a moralist or a preacher. Yet here is an area, where mankind has from the very first distinguished between acts that are right and acts that are wrong. Standards may change, but the distinction has never been obliterated. If the individual is not willing to make it for himself, society will insist on making it for him, and will compel him to conform in its own self-defense. It is not the business of the scientist to pass judgments of value in such an area as this, but judgments must be passed and will be passed. There are better ways and worse ways of handling the elemental fact of sex.

So again, I invited to the Divinity School at Harvard a little while ago one of the most distinguished chemists of our time, the recipient of a Nobel prize for his researches. He came to talk to us about the aims and methods of pure science. He was himself a man of Quaker tradition and of most delicate and sensitive conscience. "But," he said, "the moral problems which arise from the uses and abuses of my discoveries are no part of my concern as a chemist. They lie outside the province of pure science. When dealing, for example, with TNT—Trinitrotoluol—I am concerned only with the arrangement of the atoms as they combine to make up molecules, and with the resultant properties. It is none of my scientific business whether TNT is used to blow out stumps in a clearing for a cabin in a primeval forest, or to blow up men in trenches when there is a war. That may become my problem as a human being, but it is not my problem as a chemist, and when I begin to ask such questions over my test tubes I have compromised the intellectual integrity of my research."

This has been the only ground on which pure science could stand, a ground requiring a strict delimitation of the field and task of science; and such delimitation has been the means and indeed the price of many, if not most, of the more important discoveries in the natural sciences. But scientists are now beginning to ask themselves whether civilization can afford, and whether they can continue to allow themselves, an immunity from moral responsibility for the uses to which their findings are turned. Such questions have been asked for the last few years in meetings of the British Association, and are beginning to be asked in our own American learned societies. The emergence of these questions marks the beginning of a new period in the history of the scientific method. It has been suggested that a science like chemistry may make discoveries which it becomes its duty to restrict at once to those who first know them, and then resolutely to forget. Should a science like physics, for example, assume the moral responsibility of attempting to discover and then making common property such a thing as a "death ray," if it can be found? Can man in his present state be trusted with any such knowledge? These are fresh and hard questions intruding themselves into the supposedly inviolate sanctuaries of pure science.

Meanwhile, you and I, who are probably very impure scientists, but very puzzled human beings, have to pass value-judgments and act accordingly. Indeed, our entire lives are nothing but votes of confidence in the things we think worth while. No scientist can ever prove that our appraisal is correct. No one else can prove it. A judgment of value is a private act and a venture into unverified worlds. Do you believe that on the whole truth is to be preferred to falsehood, is more worth while in itself, more likely to work in the long run, and therefore to last? This is a perfectly debatable question. The present tragic situation in Europe has been largely created by a man who believes that politically truth is less effective than lies. He has deliberately and wittingly assigned the greater strategic value to falsehood, and for five years has profited by so doing. The problem is, can the people who still believe that nations should tell the truth rather than tell lies, wait him out? His short bargains with history have succeeded. What about his long-term investment?

Or take another area, that instinctive, intuitive belief in other men, which we all must have if we are to live with them. I have a friend who divides the men whom he knows into two simple classes; those with whom he would go tiger hunting and those with whom he would not go tiger hunting! It is on the whole a useful distinction. How are you to know who the men are with whom you would go tiger hunting? As you get on with life, with its human interchanges and frictions, it becomes more and more necessary to distinguish the men whom you can trust from the men whom you cannot trust. There is, so far as I know, no psychological test, measurement, or analysis which can give you any final certainty on this elemental matter. You have to rely on your deep and wholly irrational instincts as to men, to help you pass these absolutely essential judgments of value. With a native insight and instinct Jesus of Nazareth passed again and again those votes of confidence or of no confidence in the men and women he met. Before a simple universal problem like this the specialized knowledge of the natural sciences is helpless. Even the latest and most acute measurements of psychology cannot give us the certainty we would like. Nevertheless there are some men in whom we "believe."

So, also, of the ends to which one devotes one's life: money, pleasure, power, learning, art, philanthropy. Who is more nearly right about what is worth while in life, the drunk in the gutter or the Salvation Army officer who helps him up, sobers him off and tries to find him a job? Every hour of every day we are, as it were, going to the ballot box of life and casting our vote as to what we think most worth while.

In this adventure we have to appeal the case from scientific knowledge to other guides and helpers. The artists help us more here, as do the philosophers, the prophets, the saints of history. They have carried the appraisal farther than we have yet carried it, and so long as they continue to tell us that there are things in the world of more value than to eat and drink and be merry because tomorrow we die, we cannot ever be quite at rest with that which matters less.

Faith, then, is in this aspect, a quest for values and a passing of values. And religion's claim to distinction lies in its bold affirmation that it knows and affirms the truest values in life. It says that to gain the whole world and lose one's own soul is not worth while. It says that the greatest thing in the world is charity and challenges us to prove the contrary. All such pronouncements, and these are the characteristic pronouncements of our religion, are judgments of value passed by faith.

V

And finally, let us admit that the act of believing, whether it be an intellectual venture into the mysteries by which we are surrounded or the passing of moral judgments by which we distinguish that of more worth from that of less worth, involves us in risk. It may be that in vexing our minds with the ultimate nature of things we are presumptuous and invite defeat and tragedy, as did Icarus when flying toward the sun. It may be that all the poets, painters, prophets, heroes, martyrs, have been self-deceived and have sacrificed the easy animal pleasures of life about which there is no question to the quest of higher pleasures which are only illusions. These things may be so. The scientists do not know, and their kind of knowledge cannot help us here.

In one of the most famous passages of Christian theology, that in which he describes the "wager," Blaise Pascal compares faith to betting.

God is, or is not [he says]. To which side shall we incline. Reason can determine nothing about it. But you must wager; this depends not on your will, you are embarked upon the affair. Let us weigh the gain and the loss in choosing heads that God is. If you gain, you gain all; if you lose, you lose nothing. Wager then unhesitatingly that he is.

This is strong meat for many a person who thinks the analogy filled with danger. But it is more nearly right than the too prudent and reasonable attitude of a man who will venture nothing until he is assured in advance. Religion is, therefore, as some one has bluntly put it, "betting your life that there is a God," with all the risks involved in that tremendous wager.

One question must have occurred to you as we have been thinking of these things. If God, goodness, immortality, are the great realities and the values most worth while, why are they not made more plain and indubitable? If they matter so much why is there so great space for doubt still left? Heaven forbid that we should pretend to pluck the heart out of this dark matter. Yet simple human analogies, and these are the best base from which to launch our thought into the mystery, do furnish some suggestions here.

If our religion, that is, our conscious relation to God, is to be for us a real and precious thing, we must have on our side some initiative, some responsibility. You often read in European papers that "a marriage has been arranged between M and N." You think with a certain pity of two young people who may have had nothing to say in the matter. They may be in love, but quite as likely they are not in love. In either case their parents have made all the arrangements for them and they have had no say in the matter. It is not so among us in America. We expect to do our own falling in love and our own marrying. So, if you were to read in letters of fire in the sky that a religion had been arranged for God and yourself, some native independence in you would reassert itself and you would say, "No, an arrangement like that cannot be a religion for me. I must have some say in the finding and making of my own religion." God might conceivably have so well ordered these affairs that what must now be matters of faith would have been from the first matters of certain knowledge, needing no verification, calling for no risk or adventure. He might have

made it all as clear as the multiplication table and thus
have saved us the persistent uncertainty and the recurring doubts which always have attended and apparently
must attend religion. He might have done all this, and
we should then have had no alternative but to bow
before the self-evident fact and accept it. But most of
the value of the religious relationship would have been
destroyed at the outset of any such arrangement. A
religion of that kind would be all his and none ours;
and apparently religion, like friendship and love, is a
relation in which the stake of each partner is real and
first-hand. If you think twice about it you will see that
none of the values which make our personal relations
precious to us could attach to such a divine arrangement in our behalf. Our sense of the reality of life
comes from the conviction that our lives are our own
and that we have the power to do with them as we
will. Take away the risks that go with our freedom and
you have reduced us again to the level of slaves, you
have cut at the assurance that our sense of the reality
of life derives from our belief in our liberties. We
might go on, in some subservient and docile state,
with the motions of living, but firsthand life would be
gone. The reality of religion is bound up with the
reality of our own contribution to this high friendship
which we have with God. No, we will have no religion
which is "arranged" for us, even though the price of
that renunciation be the doubts and uncertainties and
risks which attend the act of faith.

Chapter III

PRAYER

WE HAVE DESCRIBED RELIGION AS THE TERM USED TO CONNOTE THE RELATIONSHIP BETWEEN GOD AND MAN. This relationship assumes that there are concerns shared by its two partners. In the broad sense of the word the life of religion consists of thoughts which are shared by God and man and actions which are shared.

Religion has never been able to obliterate the distinction between thought and action, although it has often attempted to do so. In spite of every effort to make the religious life a consistently single thing in its texture and quality, an interior contrast is felt, and is expressed in the classical language of Christian piety as that between the contemplative life and the active life.

It is worth while noticing that religion and theology did not invent this distinction. This distinction has always been there as a felt difference within our own experience and as a temperamental contrast which may be observed between individuals. Some persons are naturally more interested in thinking than in doing. Other persons are more themselves when they are busy in the world of action and affairs. The latest sciences

64

of the mind are familiar with this distinction, and for at least one of the two or three greatest psychologists of our time, Professor Jung, the difference between the "introvert" and the "extravert" is the most important initial means of understanding and classifying human beings. But Jung has not discovered a new set of facts, he has simply coined new terms for identifying old facts with which we have long been familiar.

We might pause in passing to say that we have here a good example of a situation which we often meet. The facts with which science deals have always been there. More than this, they have had names. What science does is to give its more accurate names and descriptions to facts that have been only half understood by less accurate names. This is particularly true of human facts. Science is constantly taking imperfectly named facts to court to get their names changed and brought up to date. The introvert and the extravert are not new persons, who have appeared for the first time in the twentieth century; they are persons long familiar to the human community who have got a court order to wear new names which describe them better. Here, then, are two religious types, with two different ways of living the life of religion which we share with God. To their two antithetical concerns religion has given the simple titles, Prayer and Work. These words have to cover a wide range of facts and to do heavy duty; but they serve as well as, or better than, any other two words which are available. They are sometimes paraphrased as Worship and Service.

I

Granted that we believe there is a God and that he is forever active in his world, sustaining the order of nature and concerned with the course of history, the average American, by virtue of his culture and temperament, can probably understand religion better in the terms of work than of prayer. We are a busy and energetic people. Our wits and skills have been devoted thus far to subduing a new continent, to developing its resources, to building up its now characteristic institutions. I should say that the automobile is, at the moment, the most characteristic familiar expression of the American genius. Our motor industry stands well ahead of any other in inventiveness, precision, and efficient production. We are, as the people of no other country in the world are, at home with the machine, happy in the making and the marketing of it. But this characteristic machine is the concern of an extraverted mind; it is built and used by the Sons of Martha. You must not ask too many questions about what uses we make of it. The cars we make are, for the most part, better than the rides we can take! So a meditative friend of mine from the Old World stood by a crowded American street packed with cars at the evening rush hour and said, reflectively, "Each one of them going somewhere, and all together going no-where." In our happy busy world, it is hardly good form to say such things. We are not as a people mentally at ease and at home with reflective second thoughts. In general, in so far as the typical American has a religion, it is that kind of religion which is most naturally and best expressed by work. This is not a disparagement of ourselves, or of the work we do. It is simply a matter of the correct classification of ourselves.

I had occasion a year or so ago to read with some care a number of the classical books of Christian devotion. Most of them have to do with meditation, retirement from the world, fasting, long vigils, and the like. When I passed on from these older books of Catholic Europe in the Middle Ages to our own John Woolman's *Journal*, I felt like a traveler in strange lands who had at last come home. "Building houses suitable to dwell in," he says, "preparing Cloathing suitable to the Climate and Season, and food convenient, are all duties incumbent upon us. And under these general heads are many branches of business in which we may venture health and life as necessity may require." It is in such terms that the realistic, home-spun Christianity of this American Quaker expressed itself.

In the same spirit I have been accustomed to say to each entering Freshman class at Harvard at the opening chapel service of the academic year, that a student's religion will be first and best expressed in his regular college work. He is supposedly there to study and it is in the terms of his grades that his world will take its measure of his faithfulness, his honesty, his diligence, as well as his ability. If he fails in the religion of the curriculum he cannot expect to make good some other kind of religion expressed in extracurricular ways. This I regard as sound American Protestantism.

So in our typical church we say to the doctor and the lawyer and the business man, "Your religion will express itself most naturally, and probably most truly, in your day's work. Your religion ought to be the heart of your work—the reason for which you do it and the spirit in which you do it. If there is no religion in your work, you cannot expect to achieve religion in your idle hours and your off time." A doctor trying to save a patient with pneumonia, a surgeon cutting out a malignant growth, a lawyer fighting for good government in a corrupt city, a farmer raising wheat, a fisherman hauling his trawl at sea, a teacher patiently educating the next generation, these and many other such are all doing what deserves to be called God's work in the world. They are entitled to know that this is so and should be encouraged to think of their work in this way. You do not have to be a minister or a missionary to be a person with a religious lifework. The forms of that lifework are as many as the needful occupations of all sorts and conditions of men. It is in some such ways as these that the average American, by virtue of his temperament and the whole trend of our culture, most naturally conceives of religion. If you believe in God at all, and therefore need and can find a religion, you will not quarrel with my general theory that the working hours of any decent, serious life are entitled to be called God's, and religious. This is, I think, one of the self-evident truths implied in our whole American situation.

Indeed this is, perhaps, the whole twentieth-century point of view. Some years ago Mr. H. G. Wells wrote a little book called *God the Invisible King*, in which he drew a realistic and robust picture of religion at work, of religion as work. He knows that to be religious need not mean giving up the things that men must do as their bread-labor and turning the six days of the week into perpetual Sundays with nothing but psalm-singing. All that is needed is a new temper and direction in the best work of the modern world.

The Kingdom of God is to be in the teaching at the village school, or in the planning of the railway siding of the market town, in the mixing of the mortar at the building of the workman's house. . . . There is no act altogether without significance, no power so humble that it may not be used for or against God, no life but can orient itself to him. To realise God in one's heart is to be filled with the desire to serve him, and the way of his service is neither to pull up one's life by the roots nor to continue it in all its essentials unchanged, but to turn it about, to turn everything that there is in it round to his way. . . . Many men and women are already working to-day at tasks that belong essentially to God's kingdom, tasks that would be of the same essential nature if the world were now a theocracy; for example, they are doing or sustaining scientific research or education or creative art; they are making roads to bring men together, they are doctors working for the world's health, they are building homes, they are constructing machinery to save and increase the powers of men. . . . Such men and women need only to change their orientation as men will change about at a work-table when the light that was coming in a little while ago from the southern windows, begins presently to come in chiefly from the west, to become open and confessed servants of God. This work that they were doing for ambition, or the love of men, or the love of knowledge, or what seemed the inherent impulse to work itself, or for money or honour or country or king, they will realise they are doing for God and by the power of God.[1]

II

There is for most of us, then, no serious religious problem of work. It is that other aspect of religion, the contemplative side of it which traditionally bears the name of prayer, that creates the problems for us. The problem is most acute when it is met in the terms of what we commonly call "unanswered prayer." If

[1] H. G. Wells, *God the Invisible King* (New York: The Macmillan Company, 1917), pp. 105, 106, 109, 110.

the religious theory of work "works" well, the antithetical theory of prayer often does not seem to work.
What is the matter? What are we to make of prayer?
A British Chaplain General during the Great War
said that the most frequent and stubborn question
which was put to him at the front was that stated by
the friends of "Bill who did pray, but yet had his
head blowed off." If your head "gets blowed off" in
spite of your prayers, why bother to say your prayers?
What is the use of asking God for things which more
often than otherwise you do not get?

The true nature of prayer will elude us, if we think
of it merely as a device for insuring our private safety,
comfort, and success. If the life of busy and useful
action in the world may fairly be construed as a sharing
of the countless forms of God's work in and for the
world, then the life of prayer will be the whole other
half of religion, a sharing of the thoughts of God.
Nothing less than this can really satisfy all that the
word ought to mean. Thus, when a great astronomer
said that, in studying the stars, he was "thinking God's
thoughts after him," he was describing an act which
can only be called prayer. And since God's thinking
presumably did not stop with the sixth day of creation,
we may fairly say that there is such a thing as trying
to think God's thoughts with him at this present time,
as well as after him.

These are, of course, bold words: perhaps they are
rash. Who knows what God thinks? His thoughts,

says the prophet, are not our thoughts. To speak of the thoughts and purposes of God seems almost presumptuous. How recklessly men have identified the will of God with their own prejudices, preferences, and passions. The Crusaders went into battle following banners which carried the legend *Deus Vult*. The conviction that you are doing the will of God has, it is true, a tremendously steadying and strengthening effect upon your conduct. Kipling says somewhere, that there is only one thing more terrible in action than a company of desperadoes officered by a half-dozen young daredevils, and that is a regiment of Scotch Presbyterians who rise from their knees and go into battle convinced that they are about to do the will of God. But when you consider the wars of religion, the inquisitions, the cruelties that have been wrought under the banner *Deus Vult*—"God Wills"—you become cautious about adding to those brutal bigotries. You understand what Browning meant when he said that he admired, but distrusted,

> The constant talk men of your stamp keep up
> Of God's will, as they style it; one would swear
> Man had but merely to uplift his eye,
> And see the will in question charactered
> On the heaven's vault. 'Tis hardly wise to moot
> Such topics: doubts are many and faith is weak.
> I know as much of any will of God
> As knows some dumb and tortured brute. . . .
> . . . and for such reasons I plod on.

The Vicar of Saint Mary's Church—the University Church—in Oxford says that it is very hard to be patient with "the trying people who talk as though they were God's private secretaries, knowing his plans in every detail." We have all met these persons and can agree with the Vicar. Nevertheless, when you have admitted all this, and much more, as to the presumption of trying to think God's thoughts after him and with him, and as to the tremendous margin of error which has attended that effort, the fact remains that you cannot stop men from thinking, and from trying to imagine what God is thinking.

There is no single literature in the world as soberly critical of man's long, long thoughts as is the Wisdom Literature of Israel. The writer of Ecclesiastes was convinced that such thoughts are vanity. But he was also honest enough to admit that however vain man's attempt to think God's thoughts after him may be, man will go on doing it, for such is his nature and that nature cannot be denied:

I gave my heart to seek and search out by wisdom concerning all things that are done under heaven: this sore travail hath God given to the sons of men to be exercised therewith.

A later writer in the Wisdom books says, in an altogether lovely passage, that God

. . . hath given me certain knowledge of the things that

are, namely, to know how the world was made, and the operation of the elements:

The beginning, ending, and midst of the times: the alterations of the turning of the sun, and the changes of the seasons:

The circuits of the years, and the positions of the stars:

The natures of living creatures, and the furies of wild beasts: the violence of winds, and the reasonings of men: the diversities of plants, and the virtues of roots.

The way in which this writer interjects mention of "the reasonings of men" into his catalogue of the varieties and marvels of nature has always seemed to me profoundly true. A thinker ought not to be an alien to nature; he should be a part of nature. If you wish this conviction as to the naturalness of thought brought nearer to our own times, you will find it restated in those majestic lines from Wordsworth's *Tintern Abbey*:

> And I have felt
> A presence that disturbs me with the joy
> Of elevated thoughts; a sense sublime
> Of something far more deeply interfused,
> Whose dwelling is the light of setting suns,
> And the round ocean, and the living air,
> And the blue sky, and in the mind of man;
> A motion and a spirit that impels
> All thinking things, all objects of all thought,
> And rolls through all things.

You may call this poetry rather than prose, pantheism rather than true religion. Let us not quarrel about terms for the moment. The point is that you will never succeed in permanently taming and domesticating in any small and tidy world man's restless mind. Perhaps it may be presumptuous and dangerous to try to think God's thoughts with him, but nothing short of that bold endeavor is true to man. To try to keep man's thoughts cribb'd, cabin'd, and deliberately confin'd is the unnatural thing. His mind was apparently made to take these risks, and no prudential counsels or records of repeated failure will ever dissuade him from going on taking them. You will not stop mountain climbers from attempting again and again the ascent of Everest because the expeditions thus far have cost many human lives and have failed. So the excesses of religious fanatics, who have too soon and too easily identified their own bigotries and cruelties with the mind of God, will not deter wiser and soberer men from renewing the ever unrealized endeavor to think God's thoughts with him.

Let us admit, then, that the idea of religion requires a life of the mind which man shares with God, and let us revert to our simple description of religion as a matter of a relationship, as being in this respect a companionship of minds.

The mere admission of the fact of such a companionship, the acknowledgment of its existence, is prayer and is, indeed, the basis of all prayer. I some-

times think that one of the most beautiful and adequate of all the prayers I know, is that which is used
by the Breton fishermen on the coast of France, "O
God, thy sea is so great, and my boat is so small."
What more can be said, what more needs to be said?
Here is the one deepest thought most constantly in
the minds of simple and devout men who go down to
the sea in ships; the first and last truth of their lives
stated in the homely terms of their livelihood. That
brief sentence is much more truly prayer than, let us
say, a petition that we pass an examination, or win a
war. It is not a request for any concrete happening; it
is the direct statement of an elemental truth that
compasses the whole content and conduct of life.

Those of us who are interested in philosophy often
find ourselves wondering whether there is any difference between philosophy and religion, whether indeed
philosophy does not, with persons of a reflective frame
of mind, subtly replace religion. There is one difference, and that a very important difference, which has
been pointed out by my colleague, Professor Hocking.
Philosophy, in so far as it has occasion to refer to
God, speaks of God as "he." Religion, on the other
hand, always speaks to God as "thou." The direct
and intimate second person which religion uses implies a personal relationship, which philosophy need
not admit. It is perfectly possible to concede the
existence of a God with whom one does not have any
relation. Such a God will be termed, "he." But when

that "he" is replaced by "thou," you have passed from philosophy to religion. You may remember the story told of Voltaire, that walking one day with a friend they met a Eucharistic procession. As the procession passed Voltaire lifted his hat. "But," said the friend, "I did not know that you bowed to the existence of God." "We bow," said Voltaire, "but we do not speak." The philosopher bows to God; the religious man speaks to God.

Therefore, whenever you find yourself saying "O God, thou . . ." you are a religious man who is already saying his prayers. On this basis, many of the Psalms must be described as prayers. When the Psalmist says, "I will say of the Lord, he is my refuge and my fortress," he is, perhaps, philosophizing. But when he says, more directly, "Lord, thou hast been our dwelling place in all generations," he is praying. Only some such inclusive description can cover the many elaborated kinds of prayer with which we are familiar. What comes after the simple statement "O God, thou . . ." may be thanksgiving or praise, petition or confession; it may be a mere recital of facts, facts familiar both to God who hears and him who prays. These details are secondary. What matters before all else is an awareness of a meditative side of life consciously lived in the presence of God, "unto whom all hearts are open, all desires known, and from whom no secrets are hid." Once again, the source and base of all prayer may be found in those simple words which I have already quoted to you, "O God, thy sea is so great, and my boat is so small."

III

If you look over the length and breadth of the many experiences which have been gathered under the name of religion, you will find that men have construed differently the nature and probable intention of that relationship.

The life of man is often compared to a tidal river, the nature of God to the sea. They meet at the river's mouth. Which way does the tide set at that meeting place? Arthur Hugh Clough speaks of experiences in which the incoming tide from the sea fills the river emptied at its ebb: "Far back through creeks and inlets making, comes, silent, flooding in the main." But Tennyson speaks of other experiences in which the outgoing river seems to lose itself in the ocean: "When that which drew from out the boundless deep turns again home." When we think of religion, and more particularly when we try to pray, which of these ideas is uppermost in our minds, the thought of added strength and peace coming in to us, or of our lives being given back to God?

You will say, and you are right in so saying, that we ought to have both ideas in mind. Yet there is in the long history of religion, as there is in the moral outlook of any one man over his lifetime, a less mature

and a more mature attitude toward this option of getting or giving. For example, one of my friends says
that most of us begin life wondering whether the
world is good enough for us, but grow up to wonder
whether we are good enough for the world. Matthew
Arnold put the same general idea of this shift of
emphasis in another way, when he said that the older
he grew the less he cared about his rights and the
more he cared about his duties. To be concerned
primarily for our own rights is an immature moral
trait which we all recognize in ourselves; to begin to
think soberly about our duties is to have begun to
grow up ethically.

Now, if you take the history of religion as it unfolds
over many centuries, you can discern this shift of
emphasis. When we first meet man in conscious relation to his gods, he is like a willful child, his head full
of his own plans and purposes, and intent by hook or
crook to get the help of the gods for his private proj-
ects. He wants his god to send rain on the parched
ground, to give him a good crop, to make his flocks
bear, to give him victory over his enemies. He has
various rites which are supposed to work on the god
automatically. If he says the correct words in the
correct way and does the ceremonial acts correctly—
or gets a professional person to do these things for
him in case he does not know the ritual secrets—then
the god must come to his help. It is rather like knowing the combination of a safe. Meanwhile the concep-

tion of God lying behind these primitive ideas is that of a superior power which, if rightly handled, may be coerced and exploited for our own purposes. The name for this primitive and immature conception of religion is "magic."

Now just as there are in the human world persons who remain immature all their lives, so this strain of immaturity in religion persists and keeps cropping up in even these latest times. We are very far from having outgrown the magical attitude toward religion, and there are many persons who never think of God or say their prayers unless they want some outside help for their own devices. Indeed more than one modern scholar seems inclined to think of God primarily as a power that can be used for human ends, and of what we call religion as the sum of our ways of making use of him. But however refined and sophisticated our use of God and our ways of using him, when this idea of use is uppermost, then we are in the general area which is known as magic, and the person who practices religion in this way is a magician.

At the other extreme is a much more mature and unselfish conception of the relationship; not that God is there to do things for us, but that we are here to do things for him. One of the most familiar statements of this type of religion—for us its classic statement—is to be found in the words of Jesus, "Nevertheless, not my will, but thine, be done." Religion, so construed is the admission that there is something afoot in the universe more important than our own wishes and plans. It is an effort to find out what that is and to give oneself to it. For spiritually grown-up persons, prayer is therefore primarily a mental and moral discipline by which they attempt to discover what the divine affair is, and then to conform to it. This is the conception of religion which underlies the familiar words of Jesus about losing life and finding it. He who tries above all else to save himself will lose that self. But he who is willing to lose himself in something greater and better than himself will find satisfactions that selfishness can never give him. In the broadest sense of the word we all know what this experience of losing oneself is, and how satisfying that experience can be. The wretched hours of life are those when in idleness and indecision we say, "What shall I do with myself?" The contented hours are those when we have forgotten ourselves in something outside ourselves which wholly absorbs all our attention and care. It may be reading a novel, or watching a play, or listening to music. It may be doing a piece of work in which we are interested. It may be serving some cause for which we have enlisted. When the momentary or continued act of self-forgetfulness is past we look back and realize how happy we were and what a good time we have had. Now, farther down that quite familiar road lies religion with its conviction that we are most truly happy when we believe that at some point or other we have found out what God wishes and have aligned our lives with his. Matthew Arnold says that the greatest line in all poetry is that of Dante's which reads, "In His will is our peace." As against magic, the name that we give to this kind of religion is "mysticism."

These two antithetical ideas, then, are the opposite poles of the religious relation. Magic is the attempt to get God to do our will, mysticism is our best endeavor to find and do God's will. There is no doubt which of the two is the nobler. The mystic is religiously a more mature man than the magician.

Our common human experience can help us understand these matters. We begin life with the natural self-will of children. We go on into youth with its intense self-consciousness and affectation of self-reliance. We find by hard and disappointing rebuffs that people will not always do for us what we think they ought to do, that there are other stubborn human wills in the world, as stubborn as our own. We are at first angry and baffled that we cannot always have our own way, but slowly we learn how much self-control and self-denial are necessary if we are to live with other people. We come to the time when we have to decide what we will do for a living and then we must choose between treating the world as something which we can raid for our own profit, or as being the scene of creative human endeavors at which we can lend a hand. We have to decide whether we are going to make of our lives a business of getting things for ourselves or of giving ourselves to causes that are interesting enough and great enough to absorb us and satisfy us. Then we go on to think about life and the world as a whole. Is this life of man merely "a tale told by an idiot, full of sound and fury, signifying nothing," does life in the end merely "light fools the way to dusty death?" Are our three score years and ten just a bad joke, cruel and insensitive in its forms, which existence plays on us? Or are there aspects of truth and beauty and goodness which endure and which are worth serving at any cost and all costs? Each of us learns humbly to say what a great scientist once said, "I observe that the universe is not much affected by my likes or dislikes." We make our peace with that fact and, facing about, try to discover what are its permanent likes and dislikes. All this educating and redirecting of our minds and desires and wills, belongs properly under the great heading of prayer. Prayer, so construed, is the whole meditative, thinking, feeling side of life deliberately kept open toward God. Praying stops only when we close our mental doors and windows against God, and when we say stubbornly that we do not wish or care to know what God is trying to do and what he would like us to do.

I have deliberately spent the better part of the hour in this attempt to enlarge our conception of prayer, because I am certain that most of the difficulties which attach to the idea and the practice of prayer arise from much too meager theories as to what prayer really is. To pray is, as I have just said, to keep the whole thoughtful part of life open on its Godward side. But here, as in the rest of life, the general truth needs concrete statement. Therefore, though we may truly say that we can be praying when we are studying, or thinking about our lifework, or practicing our profession, we shall not fail, in the old-fashioned phrase, to "say our prayers" as well. One of the ways, certainly, to give reality and naturalness to the idea of prayer which I have been proposing is to have the unconventional courage to say our prayers anywhere, at any time—just when we happen to feel like it. It is a mistake to confine saying our prayers to our bedsides and our churches. For example, we ought to have the spontaneity, when we are outdoors and the day is lovely, to say in so many words, "O God, I thank thee for the beauty of this day and of thy world"—or to say when we settle down indoors to a piece of hard work, "O God, this is thy work that I am doing, help me to do it well." The courage of just such informality is one of the ways to give greater reality to the thoughtful half of the religious life. If we are not natural enough and spontaneous enough to do such little acts as these, then prayer will be in danger of becoming cold, formal, occasional, and in the end forgotten and neglected. Something of all this lies behind one of the most beautiful recorded prayers in all Christian history, that of General Sir Jacob Astley before the Battle of Edgehill, "O Lord, thou knowest how busy

I must be this day. If I forget thee, do not thou forget me."

IV

Now, it is when you begin to "say your prayers" in so many words that what we call the "problem of prayer" arises. I wish to deal with that problem briefly, in conclusion. But before coming to this problem of prayer, it is worth while to realize that even among the prayers which we do say there are many which raise no problems, other than the basic problem as to whether we are in any relation whatsoever to a God who "hears" our prayer.

There is, to begin with, the familiar prayer of confession and penitence: "We have done those things which we ought not to have done and have left undone those things which we ought to have done." Every honest person knows that this is true of himself, and the better he is the more keenly he is aware of the fact. To pretend otherwise is to be a fool or a prig. There is no problem of prayer here. So with the prayers of praise and adoration. These are the prayers which are prompted by wonder, by the mood one feels, gazing at mountains or the sea or the stars—a reverent adoration of majestic and lovely things. He must be a very dull and lifeless man who is not again and again stirred to lift up his mind and heart to the beauties of the natural world. Beyond the beauties of nature is the beauty of holiness recognized in the humble and glad wonder begotten by good men and women. These point on to God. There is no problem of prayer in our praise and adoration. Furthermore we have the prayers of thanksgiving. The older we grow the more we say such prayers. For there is a problem of good in the world as well as a problem of evil, and from the standpoint of dispassionate reason, the margins of good which come to us are just as hard to explain as the margins of evil. It is not of our private merit that we here today are not among the suffering millions of Europe and Asia. We cannot preen ourselves with any self-righteousness, and as we look about the wider world where there is perplexity and pain we can only be humble and say, with Bunyan, "There, but for the grace of God, go I." It was a happy girl who once said to me years ago, "I don't understand what people mean by the problem of prayer. I have only one prayer, that of thanksgiving for all life means to me." Her prayer had not, could not have, any problems. Here again is a kind of prayer which is non-problematical. Even within the boundary of formal prayer it is our failure to confess, to adore, to praise, to give thanks which is responsible for our habit of complaining so constantly about the problem of unanswered prayer. If we are concerned that our prayers shall always be answered, it will be well for us to remember the great words in the Book of Proverbs, "God answereth him in the joy of his heart."

I come in conclusion to the area in which problems do arise; to what are technically called prayers of petition and intercession. Petition is asking God things for ourselves; intercession is asking God things for other persons. The things for which we ask may be concrete and material: success in an examination, getting a position, the cure of some disease, making money, the election of our candidate. They may be inward and spiritual: peace of mind, hopefulness, happiness.

It is sometimes said that, since mankind does not seem to have been uniformly successful in getting all the material things it has prayed for, we had best take a lesson from the book of experience and pray for spiritual things which are perhaps more sure of being had. One notices in many modern prayers a tendency to ask for what are called spiritual blessings, rather than material benefits. A still further possible solution of the so-called problem of prayer would be to give up petition and intercession altogether, as being so uncertain an area of prayer as to be best left uncultivated. More than one counsellor says, in praying don't ask for anything in particular and then you won't be disappointed. He may justify his advice by pointing out that, asking for concrete things, we are least like the mystics and the most like the magicians. He will remind us that magic doesn't always work, indeed that in the end it breaks down altogether. Your god fails to answer, and as in the old story in the Bible, you say, "Perhaps he is sleeping, or on a journey." Then when repeated insistent demands fail to get a response you come to the disappointing conclusion that he is not there at all, that there is no god. Every minister is familiar with the parishioner who says, "I prayed long and earnestly and in good faith. My prayers were not answered. Therefore I can only conclude that there isn't any God, or if there is, he does not hear and answer prayer."

Let us admit that there is a problem here, more often than otherwise felt in times of trouble as a poignant personal problem. But let us also in all candor admit that it would be a wild world if every one of us had the power to get all his petitions and intercessions answered. The head-on collisions of countless mutually exclusive prayers would blow the world to pieces in no time. The towns of Concord and Sudbury outside Boston lie in low marshy country. The Concord minister once came in to a minister's meeting in Boston and found the assembled company praying for rain. He said, "You ministers in Boston the moment a tulip begins to wilt in your front garden start praying for rain and you don't stop until all Concord and Sudbury are two feet under water."

It is quite clear that if man had actually the magical power to manipulate nature in behalf of his own desires and plans, the stability and uniformity of the world, which furnish the permanent background and setting for human life, would be destroyed. It is true that the world of nature does not always bend to our

private wishes, and there are times when we resent
that fact. But her impersonal and catholic order, when
we think twice about it, furnishes the only possible
scene for the life of all sorts and conditions of men.
On sober second thought few of us would wish to
have the power to coerce nature in our private behalf.
Our sense of the reliability of the world in which we
live would be destroyed and we should thereafter live
in fear of what some rival and possibly more powerful
magician might do against us and to our hurt.

So, also, with the affairs of other men which are
the substance of intercession. Here we come into an
area where mind as well as matter is at stake, and
where the subtle influence of one human mind upon
another is a powerful and incalculable factor. What
happens and what may happen in this area no one
knows. I once heard a very distinguished theologian
try to rationalize intercessory prayer as a kind of
thought transference or power of suggestion, by which
one human mind acts directly on another. Most of us
would shy away from this dubious explanation of our
intercessions for others. To assume such responsibility
in the control of another's life would be a terrible risk
and responsibility. It would fall in that kind of de-
bated area where the doctors discuss the wisdom of
euthanasia, i.e., the practice of painlessly killing in-
curable patients before nature takes their lives. Medicine is unwilling to assume any such responsibility. So,
I think, even could we be persuaded that there were

available some subtle spiritual energy, expressing itself as prayer, by which we could control and direct the lives of others, as a man at a switchboard can steer an unmanned boat, we should shrink from the prospect. Most psychologists would say that any such attempt is mentally and morally unsafe. They insist that the patient must co-operate in his own cure, his will must go with the mind of the physician. This is sound Christianity; Saint Paul writes to Philemon that he wishes his goodness to be of his own free will and not of necessity. We have no moral right to tamper with the souls of others by anything like psychic means. Any attempt to exercise such control by prayer is a subtle attack on the basic conception of moral goodness and therefore on the stable foundations of human character.

On this whole subject we can only fall back upon the profound and accurate insights which we have in Lincoln's Second Inaugural. Speaking of North and South he said, "Both read the same Bible, and pray to the same God; and each invokes his aid against the other. The prayers of both could not be answered—that of neither has been answered fully." One gathers from these words that, even had he believed he had any such power, Lincoln would not have coerced the South by his prayers. There is no least residue of magic in Lincoln's religion. Therein lay its true greatness. When he said, as is reported of him, that he was more anxious that he and the North should be

on God's side, than that God should be on his side,
he spoke as a spiritually mature man, as a mystic
rather than a magician.

We apparently have not, then, in prayer any magical and mechanical means of exploiting nature in our
own behalf or of bending other men to our desire and
will, even for their own good. And if we think we
have such power and make the exercise of that supposed power the test of the efficacy of prayer, we are
bound to be confronted with the problem of unanswered prayer. In the end we shall probably be driven
to loss of faith in any kind of prayer, in all religion,
and in God. That has been the experience of the race
thus far, a slow and painful realization of the final
futility of coercive prayers.

Something of this conclusion is anticipated in the
words of Jesus in the story of the temptation: "Thou
shalt not tempt the Lord thy God." What do those
words about tempting God mean; how can we tempt
God? Jesus meant, "Thou shalt not make trial of God
upon thine own terms, for thine own designs." In the
immediate instance of that story, Thou shalt not leap
from a pinnacle of the temple, and expect God to
suspend for thee the operations of his laws.

Preaching upon the text one Sunday many years ago
in the Harvard Chapel I was stressing the importance
of not using our prayers as a kind of magic by which
to coerce God to do what we wished, I was saying
that we should not put God to such tests. After the

service President Lowell said to me, in substance, "I think you were in danger of overworking your idea. When we pray to God we ought to ask for what is on our minds and in our hearts. If we begin to introduce self-consciousness and a critical choice of subjects into our prayers they will become unnatural and therefore unreal. It is true that we shall not get all we ask; no boy expects to get from his father all he asks, but that does not prevent his going on asking. A child ought to be made to feel that he is quite free to come and ask for anything he wants, leaving the matter then to his father's wisdom and decision. His father will give him some of the things he asks for and will not give others. So, in prayer, it is not essential or important that we get everything we ask for. What matters is that when we come to God we should be natural and spontaneous and honest, should in short be ourselves. A sense of the reality of the relationship implied by prayer, and of absolute freedom in that relationship, is more important than the particular consequences of prayer. Therefore, I think that at any given moment we should ask God for what we really want, even though we realize that he may not grant it."

I have always been grateful to Mr. Lowell for those wise words. They seemed to me then, and still seem to me in retrospect, to put the problem in its right perspective. Our relationship to those we love and with whom we live in this human world is more important than any or all of the concrete benefits we get from the relationship. It is the free communion of open minds and the free play of open hearts that we must defend before all else. Otherwise every friendship and affection drops to the level of a bargain counter where we may get a good trade, but nothing more. The child learns as he grows what he ought to ask for. His own experience criticizes and disciplines the nature of his request of his father. He can look back, at a later day, and see that at times he asked for wrong things which were not given him and were rightly withheld. Meanwhile he has kept unimpaired, through the slow education of his wants and desires, the comradeship and the love of a son and a father. This has survived his childish resentment that he did not always get what he asked for, and he sees that it was the love and companionship that mattered most and lasted longest, whatever the ratio between things granted and things denied.

The deeper truth of both our petitions for ourselves and our intercessions for others lies somewhere in this simple analogy. There are some things you may selfishly want which you know instinctively are not right subjects for prayer. You cannot with good conscience ask God for them. Therefore they are left unsaid in prayer. The process of religious self-criticism and self-discipline has already begun with the admission of this necessity of leaving many a natural desire out of prayer. Meanwhile there are other wishes and purposes which do not seem, by their nature, excluded from what might well be God's thought and will; these we may properly pray for. Such prayers may be answered; they may go unanswered. But whether answered or unanswered, we ought to keep through the whole experience our untroubled assurance that our communion with God is real and that, for better or for worse, we must in his presence always be ourselves. If it be true that our relation to God is prior in importance to all the concrete gains we get from it, then unanswered prayers are not a reason either for giving up praying or for losing faith in God. What should persist through it all is our steady endeavor to think God's thoughts after him, and with him—a keeping of the whole thoughtful side of life open toward him. The purest petition for ourselves which we can conceive might, therefore, be those words of the Psalm, "Let the words of my mouth and the meditations of my heart be alway acceptable in thy sight, O Lord my strength and my redeemer."

Chapter IV

MORALS

THE ENGLISH WORD "MORALS" COMES FROM THE
LATIN "MOS"—PLURAL, "MORES"—MEANING CUSTOMS
or manners. When we wish to parade a little learning
we sometimes speak, even in English, about the
"mores" of a people; that is, the general patterns of
their behavior. Automobiles and radios, compulsory
education for all children, colleges for many of our
youth, state highways with their white lines and traffic
lights, some kind of restrictions on gambling and drink-
ing and free love, are all part of the "mores" of
America. These are the ways we live together.

Since the word "morals" tends to revert to this
basic idea of custom, and since customs are generally
thought of as secular rather than religious, persons
who are concerned to maintain a connection between
morals and religion, are apt to use the other word
which so often appears in this connection, the word
"ethics." It is the present practice to speak more often
of "the Christian ethic" than of "Christian morals."
If the change is intended to indicate a desire to emphasize the importance of clear ideas of right and
wrong in this connection then it may be warranted.
But, so far as origins are concerned, there is no special

gain in substituting the one word for the other. If the word "morals" comes from Latin, the word "ethics" comes from the Greek—*ethos*—and means precisely the same thing. In the latter language the "ethics" of a people is simply their manners.

And at this point even so competent a book as the Oxford English Dictionary knocks a single idea back and forth, like a tennis ball, between the Latin and Greek courts on the two sides of the net. "Ethics," we find, is "the science of morals." "Moral," we read in turn, means "ethical, involving ethical praise or blame." We shall do well, therefore, to remember that behind both words, morals and ethics, there lies the basic conception of social custom, men's settled and agreed upon ways of behaving.

I

We have at Harvard a department known as "Social Ethics." I once heard the greatest scholar whom I have ever known ask a student who was being examined in the field whether there was any ethics that was not social. The student hesitated and the professor gave the answer, "No. All ethics, by the very idea at stake, must be social." We sometimes use the term "private morals"—but that does not imply the habits of a hermit. It merely denotes ways in which the individual behaves in those areas of conduct not yet laid out in recognized patterns. Robinson Crusoe on his island could hardly be said to have had any morals or ethics so long as he was alone. Morality and ethics made their appearance when he found Man Friday. I am ignoring for the moment the fact that even in his solitude Crusoe had a relation to God. But in general and as a social science which, left to itself, need not necessarily invoke the idea of God, our subject concerns the interrelations of men living together.

There has been from the first an instinct in the herd to protect itself against those forms of conduct which make of the unassimilated individual a problem or a burden. You cannot let a murderer wander around loose. If you don't kill him you must at least shut him up or send him away. The will to live prompts you to fashion social customs by which you may defend yourself against him. So, today you cannot allow a man with smallpox to move about at will among his fellows. You may care for him tenderly, but you must isolate him for the time being. Again, in these days when your nation is riddled with spies, *agents provocateurs,* paid propagandists and incendiary revolutionists from cultures quite other than your own, you have a right to compel a man to identify himself and give an account of himself. The customs of your country ought to be safeguarded against those who would bore from within and scuttle the ship of state. In countless ways the group as a whole, in the interests of the many who make it up, will take affairs into its own hands and when laws are wanting to protect it from the antisocial conduct of the individual it will make such laws. The "mores" of a particular group may be higher or lower, anywhere from the instincts of a hunting pack to the rules of a religious order. But once the necessity of some agreed upon practice is felt, the group will fashion its codes of customs, manners, morals, ethics.

Now these social patterns, formulated in law, are mainly concerned with the things the individual may not do. What he may do, "inside the law," is left for the most part to his own devices. Meanwhile morality gets a bad name because it is felt to be so negative. Thus one of the familiar classical codes of morals is the Ten Commandments. Most of those commandments, as you know, begin with the prohibition, "Thou shalt not." That negative, strong as it is in English, is not nearly as strong as it is in Hebrew, in which one commandment after another begins, "No," and then goes on to elaborate this "No." It is the fashion today to rebel against the restrictions of the Ten Commandments and to deplore the too negative view of morality which they embody. The Old Testament, we tell ourselves, is the source of the now disparaged and despised morality of the Puritans. Hence the widespread popular idea that religion has been, and still is, the world's great kill-joy, the sum of the things you may not do. Personally, when I read the Ten Commandments, I feel very much as I do standing on the rim of the Grand Canyon, looking down into the gorge which the Colorado River has cut through the rock. It has been through the narrow and stony walls of those primal prohibitions that mankind has cut its way to whatever more open places it has later reached. The ancient prohibitions of the Decalogue remind me of that magnificent passage in the Second Book of Esdras, "Then were the entrances of this world made narrow . . . and very painful. . . . The righteous shall suffer straight things and hope for wide." As a modern writer has sagely added, "If you want to find out what the Ten Commandments are all about, just break one of them!" History knows no such thing as a human society without its Grand Canyons of stern preliminary prohibition. The permissive and gracious sanctions of every society, its opportunities for a positive and affirmative life, lie beyond and below that canyon.

In their elementary form our moral judgments are little more than registered approval and disapproval, praise and blame. But as the ideas of praise and blame become more elaborated they reappear as judgments of right and wrong, good and evil. Not a day goes by but we have to pass these judgments of right and wrong upon our own motives and proposed conduct, as upon the actions of others. Will it be right or wrong for you to cut your next class after this hour? Will it be right or wrong to take advantage of a card you have accidentally seen in your opponent's hand at a game of bridge this evening? At play and work these awkward questions are always coming up. How much simpler life would be if they didn't. How happy for us if we could follow that line of Walt Whitman's which William James used to like to quote:

I think I could turn and live with animals, they are so
    placid and self-contain'd.
I stand and look at them long and long.
They do not sweat and whine about their condition,
They do not lie awake in the dark and weep for their sins,
They do not make me sick discussing their duty to God.

But, alas, we cannot live with the animals, and our inability to do so is the price we pay for being men not beasts.

Meanwhile, as we grow up and get on, both as individuals and as a race, we become less concerned merely to avoid doing wrong and more interested in doing right. The positive rather than the negative side of morality appeals to something in us, if you will to a sublimated adventurer or creative artist. It is, thus, the mission of moral ideas to point to a goal as yet far beyond us. We all have glimpses of sincerity, honesty, kindness, patience that we have not attained. Indeed, all moral idealism leads toward and finally lands us in a dilemma, which has been bluntly stated by an English scholar, "My ethical end must at least be capable of attainment," and, "My end, just because it is an ethical end, must be incapable of attainment." We know what is meant by that contradiction, and are familiar in personal experience with what is commonly called the receding moral ideal. You may remember one of Browning's poems in which he describes himself as pursuing a fleeting figure, the hem of whose garment forever slips through his fingers just as he is about to grasp it, "Soul of mine, hadst thou clung to the vesture." Hence the peculiar fact with which the history of religion is quite familiar, that the better a man actually becomes the worse he seems to himself to be. His ideal, as he grows in character, recedes even faster than the rate of his achievement. Emerson says somewhere that the figure of Jesus can never appeal to sensual and selfish persons. As one begins to understand what is meant by purity of heart one can understand how it was that George Matheson, that saintly hymn writer, could say, "Son of Man, I have never come up with thee, modern as I am."

II

We come here to what is, I think, the most important difference between morality and religion. We are familiar with the modern person, who in these changing days has lost his belief in old religious creeds, and who says, "I try to be good, as good as I can be; why do I need religion as well?" The answer to this question is reasonably simple; the moral struggle and the religious experience are qualitatively of two different kinds. In the world of morals the goal which you set before yourself is an ideal; that is, it is not as yet actual. It has not come to pass as an achieved fact. It is something yet to be attained, fulfilled, realized. There is a distance between you and it, and even as you approach it, it will withdraw from you. There is, therefore, about what we call the moral life a constant sense of strain and effort, even the danger of exhaustion from over-effort. In the religious realm, on the contrary, that to which in religion you are united, is just as real as you are. Indeed it is more real. However unlike it you may be, you love it and you belong to it. You do not think yourself good enough to love it and belong to it, but such is the nature of your God that in spite of your lack of desert he welcomes you. That is why the word "love" is, on the whole, a better word with which to describe our relation to God than the word "friendship." Friendship is a relation between equals. Love is a relation between persons who know themselves to be unlike and who feel unequal. So, Elizabeth Barrett writes to Robert Browning, "Unlike are we, O princely heart, unlike." So, I am reminded of a college friend who wrote me years ago that he did not know what he had done to deserve such happiness, but he was engaged to the daughter of a bishop and was going to be married. If he had used the terms we are discussing he would have said that morally he could at best only aspire to the bishop's daughter, since she was beyond his deserts; but as a matter of religious fact he loved her and she seemed to love him. Again using the terms we are discussing, he would have had to say that it was his faith which had leaped the moral gap between himself and her.

The relation of love as between men and women is based upon the complex fact of a mutual likeness and a mutual unlikeness in bodily structure and function, in ways of feeling and thinking. There is enough likeness to make the relation possible, but there is enough unlikeness to give to the relation its piquancy, its problems, and its joys. It is altogether a more complicated relationship than that between friends who are equals, friends in whom likeness is so strong that it blots out unlikenesses.

Now, in some form or other, the same is true of our thought of God and our relation to him. The Bible is filled with the two contradictory ideas of man's likeness to God and God's unlikeness to man. God made man in his own image—there is this fact of a basic likeness. But it is equally true that God's thoughts are not our thoughts, nor his ways our ways—the patent unlikeness is equally true. Therefore in religion, as in the human relationship, the mind and heart shuttle back and forth between these antithetical ideas. I suppose that is one of the reasons why the symbols and language of sex have bulked so large in religion—that the word "love" which concedes the riddle of likeness and unlikeness as between the partners, is faithful to the fact.

We can understand the religious experience, if we

try to state it in some of its less theological terms. Here, for example, are the symphonies of Beethoven and Brahms. They are not moral ideals, they exist in achieved fact. They are there on the scores, with all the parts for all the instruments. They are already real. For the musician they are, if anything, more real than his own musical taste or skill. They are as real as the stars are to the astronomer. What is more he can make contact with them, hear them, play them. Something in us, as we learn a little about music, responds to them, we might even dare to say corresponds to them. When Sidney Lanier says of Beethoven,

> O Psalmist of the weak, the strong,
> O Troubadour of love and strife,
> Co-litanist of right and wrong,
> Sole Hymner of the whole of life,

he is speaking as a lover of music, indeed as a religious man who is, in these terms, a lover of God.

And yet there is always something in the symphony that eludes us, escapes us, defies us, and we put aside the score or close the program feeling pathetically the unlikeness between us and the master. How seldom do we hear a symphony or an opera perfectly conducted. It is a very rare experience, and when it comes it is, I suppose, a hint of the mystic's moment of absolute peace. Once, for example, I heard such a performance of "Tristan and Isolde." Every one present knew and felt it. The critics said next day in the papers that on the stage and backstage, the singers, the orchestra, the scene shifters and all concerned knew that something very rare was happening. That was not a moral experience, it was in its own terms a religious experience.

The question, then, "Why do I need a religion if I have a moral code?" is not easy to answer in a single dogmatic sentence. All you can say is that in the course of life we have experiences which in kind fall in the religious area rather than the moral area. In short, things happen to you in life that are not covered by the idea of morality with its perpetual straining after the ever-receding ideal, which forever gives you the slip the better you become, and moves on ahead of you.

You find, in this area, as in the world of human relations, that you have fallen in love with that which is true or beautiful or good; and that falling in love involves you in all the joy and the despair, the humility and the exaltation which this complex emotion must always breed. I cannot tell you, in so many words, therefore, why you need a religion as well as a code of morals. I can only tell you that quite apart from, and over and above, the moral struggle these other things are likely to happen to you, and when they do happen they have their own unique quality. When they happen it is the part of wisdom to know that you have come within the circle of the religious idea.

III

I should like to turn, now, for the remainder of the hour, to the more specific subject of Christian ethics. The ethics of Christianity is rooted in the morality of the Old Testament, whatever its full flower may be. There are, it is true, religions of truth and religions of beauty as against ethical religions. There have been scientists who have gone a long way toward God in their single-minded quest for truth. They have been compelled to neglect the quest for beauty, so intense has been their preoccupation with truth. Darwin's tragic confession that his devotion to science had cost him much, that if he had his life to live over again he would be at pains to read some poetry and hear some music every day, is a classic case in point. There have been artists whose passion for beauty has made them indifferent to the kind of truth which science seeks and heedless of much of our conventional morality. The problem of these nonmoral, if not immoral, geniuses in the realm of art is a familiar and a difficult one. One can only say that their neglect of truth on the one hand and goodness on the other hand has been the price they have thought it worth while to pay for their insights into beauty. We ought to add that, of itself, neglect of the moral conventions is no guarantee that one is or will ever become an artist of the first rank. The unmorality of many a great poet, painter, musician, was an incident or accident in his life, not its essence.

Meanwhile the religion of the Bible, both of the Old and the New Testaments has never been content with religion as truth or beauty. The Bible requires that goodness be included as a necessary part of religion. The Old Testament insists upon righteousness, and the New Testament insists upon love.

I think one can only say at this late date that an insistence upon goodness must be part of any religion which is to command general respect. There are not many of us who are great scientists or great artists. Our chances of discovering some unknown truth or creating a work of deathless beauty are not large. But every day of our lives we do have to decide between a better and a worse, between right and wrong. Therefore, a religion which leaves out goodness would be, for you and me, an imperfect religion, since it would ignore so great an area of our daily experience. To our private necessity we must add the grave moral issues of our whole western civilization.

There is a theory abroad that most persons begin life by being moral, and after they have attained a certain degree of goodness, graduate as it were to religion. If you are good you will finally be religious, so runs the formula. I am inclined to think that life works the other way. The probability is that most persons have experiences which may be called qualitatively religious, and then that they purify these experiences morally. This certainly seems to be what happened in Bible times. The Jews always had a religion, but it was imperfectly moral at the start and it became morally mature only as the centuries went on. The religion of the prophets is ethically a better religion than that of the judges. So, even at this latest day we are still faced with the problem whether we can make the existing religions of the world more moral than they now are. In some such prospect lies our only hope of the peace of the world.

There is no need, then, to resent or to apologize for the emphasis which the Bible, both as Judaism and as Christianity, lays upon the part which morality plays in a mature religion. It is in the terms of righteousness, of simple goodness, that you and I will most often meet religion. And although religion is in its quality a different sort of experience from the moral struggle, it does not propose to do away with that struggle. On the contrary it gives you a whole new added set of reasons for going on with the struggle and strength for the struggle, since in religion your moral goal is not some remote receding ideal, but is a reality which already exists, is God himself to whom even now you belong.

There was a time, a few years ago, when men thought that in the Gospels there was, if we would hunt long enough, a ready-made answer to all the moral problems of our modern life. To the question, "What would Jesus do?" which is a very simple way of putting the case for Christianity, the answer was, "Search the Scriptures, and ye shall know." Most of us have now given up the idea that there is already written down in the Gospels an advance answer to many of the particular problems of which modern Christians are so painfully aware. That we are under Christian bonds to love our neighbor as we love ourselves, is clear. But the forms which that love takes are manifold and often perplexing in their possible contradictions. We Christians not merely disagree on many matters of moral detail, we have to learn to disagree in charity, without reading one another out of the church and out of religious court. If you insist that private conscience is a reality and its development a duty, you cannot deny to other men the right which you claim for yourself. On the vexed moral problems which perplex us most, those of property, and sex, and the state, the organization of our industrial life, and the handling of money, there are in detail wide differences of opinion between Christians, of whose sincerity and uprightness there is no doubt. Part of our growth in the very spirit of charity consists of a willingness to differ in many of our moral judgments without ceasing to love and trust one another. To come to the point where you can say to another man, "I don't agree with you, and in this matter I think you are mistaken; nevertheless I respect and trust you," is to have got beyond the impatient mood of the inquisitor and persecutor.

Meanwhile, certain distinguishing characteristics of the Christian approach to moral problems deserve mention.

IV

There is, first of all, the question as to how Jesus thought of his own teaching, as we have it in the Gospels. For some years past there has been a popular theory that Christianity, as we first meet it in that teaching, was predominantly ethical and only incidentally religious. Jesus is said to have been interested in conduct, not in dogma. One remembers Matthew Arnold's definition of religion as "morality touched with emotion." From this inference followed a widespread attempt to identify Christianity solely with ethics and to let its supposedly meager doctrinal content go by the board. We concluded that when Christianity had dug in on its ethical lines it would be in an impregnable position from which it could not be dislodged; which indeed no one was likely to attack, since it was assumed that, whatever might be thought about Christian dogma, every one was agreed as to the validity of the Christian moral ideal. As a matter of recent history this expectation has not been realized. The Christian ethic has been more savagely assailed by states like Germany and Russia than ever Christian dogma was assailed by scientists and historians. The attack is not confined to these two nations, but is symptomatic of trends in many other lands. The Christian ethic is at this moment in a very exposed position, which is proving increasingly difficult to hold.

Meanwhile the opinion that the teaching of Jesus is ethical rather than religious has been reconsidered and revised within Christian circles, and it is now generally agreed that Jesus was before all else a religious figure, that his ethics follows from his religion, and means nothing when divorced from that religion. So Canon Barry of Westminster writes,

> Christianity is a way of life: ethical direction is inherent in it and the fruits of the Spirit are and always must be the guarantee of its claim on men's allegiance. Yet it is not primarily an ethic. We cannot have the Christian way of living apart from the Christian religion. The liberals of the late nineteenth century assumed that the Christian moral principles would always hold the allegiance of men, even though dogmatic Christianity would not survive in the climate of modernity. That genial expectation has been falsified. We cannot reconstruct the Christian ethic save on the basis of Christian faith.[1]

Personally, I entirely agree with this latest appraisal of the nature of the teaching of Jesus. Jesus was interested above all else in what he called the Kingdom (or Reign) of God and its coming on this earth, a coming by direct divine act rather than by the accumu-

[1] F. R. Barry, *Christianity and the New World* (New York: Harper & Brothers), pp. 1 ff.

lated effects of man's endeavors. All that Jesus has to say about human conduct is conditioned by his prior concern for that Kingdom.

Now there are three possible ways of construing the ethical teaching of Jesus. You may say that it was intended to improve men's behavior within the existing patterns of the Roman Empire and of Judaism, to be so much oil of patience, charity, forgiveness, and the like applied to the superheated bearings of the existing secular order. Or you may say that it was intended to be a guide to conduct during a period of drastic transition from the kingdoms of this world to the Kingdom of God, and therefore was to have only a temporary relevance. Thus, many scholars call the teaching of Jesus "the ethic of the interim." Or, finally, you may say that it is a description of the ways in which men will live together in the Kingdom, an ethic which is prophetic of a different kind of social order, and not geared to the existing secular world at hand.

It is entirely possible, and may well be probable, that the ethics of the Synoptic Gospels is of this second or third kind. Certainly, the more you read and think about the Gospels, the more radical their moral teaching seems. They take exception to our axioms rather than to our subsequent logic. They challenge our premises instead of quarreling with our conclusions. They make you think about your conduct, not at the superficial level, but at some level at once deeper and higher than that on which you are now living. So construed the Christian ethic would seem to require you to behave in ways which are divorced from or in advance of any present standards for social conduct, and, in so far as you succeed in doing so, to put you out of touch with the world at hand. That, as a matter of fact is what often happens to persons who take the Christian ethic with passionate earnestness. They find themselves at loggerheads with the accepted standards of conduct in the professions, in business, in politics and warmaking. The ethics of the Kingdom of God for example, seems to presuppose co-operation between its members; the world at large is still run by competitive processes. How to make a co-operative principle work in a society which is set up for competition is a moral riddle of the first magnitude. I have said these things to indicate that plainly the Christian ethic is something other than a handy device for oiling the machinery of a frankly materialistic social system. It is more radical than we generally realize. Perhaps this is its strength. Such is Professor Whitehead's verdict. He holds that the ethics of Christianity is impracticable at any given moment—"As society is now constituted a literal adherence to the moral precepts scattered throughout the gospels would mean sudden death"—but that this impracticable ethics is mankind's "most precious instrument of progress."

The greatness of Christianity—the greatness of any valuable religion—consists in its "interim ethics." The

founders of Christianity and their early followers believed
that the end of the world was at hand. The result was
that with passionate earnestness they gave free rein to
their absolute ethical intuitions respecting ideal possibilities without a thought of the preservation of society.
The crash of society was certain and imminent. "Imprac-
ticability" was a word which had lost its meaning . . .
A standard had now been created, expressed in concrete
illustrations, foolproof against perversions. This standard
is a gauge by which to test the defects of society. So long
as the Galilean images are but the dreams of an unrealized
world, so long must they spread the infection of an uneasy
spirit.[2]

V

Let us turn to one or two concrete aspects of this "impracticable ethic." There is, for example, the familiar
doctrine of the second mile. In the Sermon on the
Mount Jesus says, "Whosoever shall compel thee to go
a mile, go with him twain." He had in mind a military
necessity with which he and his people were often
faced. The custom of Rome allowed the army to im-
press any civilian whom it met anywhere in the
Empire, and to compel him to carry its baggage for
one mile. Using this situation as a figure of speech
Jesus said, When you have gone the mile that duty

[2] Alfred North Whitehead, *Adventures of Ideas* (New York: The
Macmillan Company, 1933), pp. 18-21.

requires, then go a voluntary second mile on your own account.

Back in the Old Testament we read, "Be not righteous overmuch; neither make thyself overwise; why shouldest thou destroy thyself?" It is true that these words are found in the rather cynical book of Ecclesiastes and do not voice the morality of the Old Testament at its best. But they do suggest what we might call the tendency of all moral systems to establish some mean level of decency which represents the average practice of a community. It is a well-recognized fact that laws ought not to get too far in advance of the standards and habits of a majority of the people; laws can only reflect and codify their usage. Laws which represent too high a standard tend to become inoperative. At any given moment in the history of a people there will be what we might call a mean high-water mark and a mean low-water mark of social custom. The morals then current will not let you fall below the low-water mark, but will not require you to rise above the high-water mark. As long as you keep within the law, which is represented by the space between low water and high water you are a decent citizen. No one has any right to complain of you and you have sufficient grounds for being satisfied with yourself. Legalism, while it prohibits the lower ranges of vice, tends to dispense with the higher reaches of virtue. Some such inference lies behind the cool and perhaps common-sense counsel of Ecclesiastes, "Be not righteous overmuch."

Now it is against precisely this quality of moral meanness in all legal systems that Jesus seems to be protesting. His theory of morality is that we should be righteous overmuch, should actually overdo the business of being good. This idea of overdoing goodness is the theme of the Sermon on the Mount, a theme which is illustrated, but not exhausted, by a number of concrete examples. Once it is launched on its course, the Sermon on the Mount says that our righteousness should exceed conventional righteousness, otherwise we cannot belong to the Kingdom of Heaven. You are not only not to kill; you are not to get angry. You are not only not to commit adultery, you are not to let your mind dwell on sensuality. You are not only not to clutter up your speech with oaths, you are to learn to tell the truth in a simple "Yes" and "No." You are not to hit back when you are hit, and you are to turn the other cheek. If a man asks your coat you are to give him that, and your overcoat as well. You are not merely to love your friends—that is natural and easy; you are to love your enemies also. The fifth chapter of Matthew ends with the sweeping injunction, "Be ye therefore perfect, even as your Father which is in heaven is perfect." That command is not, as is so often said, a counsel of impossible perfection. You are not told to be as good as God is. Goodness is not a mass, it cannot be weighed and measured by volume. Perfection is a quality and manner of life, rather than a mere massive bulk of excellence. As for the manner of God's perfection, he is not morally mean. He makes his sun rise on the evil and on the good, and sends his rain on the just and on the unjust.

I have never quite known and do not yet know just what to say about these familiar sayings of Jesus. Are they intended as literal rules to be literally followed, or are they picturesque instances of the kind of goodness expected of Christians, not to be taken too literally? If you say that we need not follow their letter, you are in danger of losing their spirit. But if you say that they are to be followed word for word, you will certainly get into difficulties in the world as it is now organized. Meanwhile the principle at stake is quite plain. You are to overdo goodness, you are to be morally better than the common level of conventional decency requires you to be.

This principle is even more plainly stated in a passage in Saint Luke's Gospel, in which Jesus says, in substance, "When, as a servant, you have come in from your day's work in the field and say, I now have done my day's work and have earned a rest, then you must be prepared to start work again waiting table in the house." "So likewise ye when ye shall have done all those things which are commanded of you, say, We are unprofitable servants: we have done that which was our duty to do." This is the most direct and unequivocal

statement in the teaching of Jesus of the basic principle of the Christian ethic. The requirements of that
ethic are not satisfied by the average of accepted
morality, as defined in the terms of the forty-hour
week. Christianity requires that of your own free will
you shall work overtime.

Apparently this marginal goodness of the Christian
is intended to introduce into any given situation a
creative energy which tends to alter that situation by
getting it onto a new and higher level. If, as Jesus
says, you love your friends who love you, what particular merit is there in that attitude and act? Everyone
does so as a matter of course. But if you love your
enemies you put into the relation between yourself
and your enemy a new factor which may entirely
change the relation. Conventional goodness so far
from requiring you to love your enemies, may encourage you to hate them, but Christian love challenges
you to try to love them, difficult as that act is to conceive and more difficult as it will be to achieve.

The best simple illustration of this principle at
work in the world of which I have any knowledge is
found in the life story of a certain Canada Blackie.
Canada Blackie was a murderer serving a life sentence
in Auburn Prison, in New York, when Thomas Mott
Osborne became warden of the prison. Osborne, fired
with his dream of the Mutual Help League within the
prison, determined to make Canada Blackie the cornerstone of his structure. At first Blackie was stubborn,

recalcitrant, rebellious and non-co-operative. But the quiet siege which the warden laid to his hardness of heart finally melted his resentment and he became the chief advocate of the new system. When, finally, Canada Blackie lay dying of tuberculosis in the warden's house he said, "There are some people that have helped me. They are not the preaching and praying kind. But there have been some people who have treated me better than I deserved, with the result that they made me better than I wanted to be or naturally would have been." That seems to me to come very near the secret of the Christian ethic. A Christian is expected to treat the world better than it deserves, with the result that the world will become better than it had planned to be or would otherwise have been if left to the mercy of some cool and calculating goodness which takes care never to overdo itself.

A passing word ought perhaps to be inserted here as to the New Testament term "love." We think of love as being the distinctive and the cardinal Christian virtue. Curiously enough it is not a word which occurs very often in the teaching of Jesus as we find it in the earlier Gospels. It belongs to the Pauline and Johannine writings. In the Synoptic Gospels the word is almost wholly confined to the recurring citation from the Old Testament about the first and the second great commandments, that we should love God and love our neighbor. True, the teaching of Jesus describes ways of conduct which can only be called loving, and the story of his life is filled with incidents which are examples of love; but it is worth while realizing that as our New Testament stands we owe the word itself to Paul and John rather than to Jesus.

Behind the word "love" as we find it in the later books of the New Testament there are in the original two different words; one which occurs often in the Fourth Gospel and means generous friendship; the other—that which Paul habitually uses—is translated in our Authorized Version as "charity." Unfortunately the word "charity" has now lost in English its original and ampler meanings, and has shrunk to meager dimensions. We now identify charity with almsgiving, contributions to philanthropies and relief funds. Plainly that is not what the original meant. If charity must now be understood to mean that and nothing more we have to find another and more accurate word. All modern translations, therefore, substitute "love" for "charity." In so doing, however, they invite the introduction into Christian thought of a whole set of ideas which, again, are no part of the original. The word "love" in English speech is most commonly associated with the emotions and the passions involved in the relation of the sexes. There was in the original language of the New Testament a third word which referred to sexual love, and that word was never used by any New Testament writer as the basis for religious symbolism. Our modern preference for the word "love" as against the word "charity" has undoubtedly bred

into the common mind a set of associations which
have nothing to do with the nature of the primal Christian virtue, and which have sentimentalized it out of
all relation to the original idea. The term agape—
which is Paul's word—is not a word which concerns
the senses or the emotions. A classical scholar who has
meditated much on an exact translation says that
whatever else the word agape may mean, it means in
the first instance "a steady set of the will." Loving
your enemy therefore is not a matter of liking him;
you cannot control your deep and instinctive likes and
dislikes at any given moment. Loving your enemy is,
in spite of what may be a deep dislike for him, a
determination to seek his good rather than his hurt.
It is an attitude and an act prompted by a sober ethical purpose. Liberal Protestantism needs sorely to get
this word "love" out of the slough of sentimentality
into which it has sunk and to set it once more upon
the hard ground of moral austerity.

VI

I come, in conclusion, to some consideration of the
major moral issue of our time, that of the theoretical
validity of the Christian ethic. This is, in the forms in
which we are now meeting it, a relatively new issue.
Men have often wondered whether Christianity was
practicable. But it is only in these last years that they
have questioned its validity as an ideal. It was in the

first quarter of the fourth century that Christianity became the official religion of the Roman Empire. Constantine published the Edict of Toleration in the year 313. From that day until this, a period of sixteen hundred years, the Western world has given lip service to the moral ideals of Christianity. No state or century or people has ever realized those ideals. The contrast between what men have professed with their lips and have done in their lives has always been sharp, and has given rise to the familiar charge that Christendom has been little better than a corporate hypocrisy over all these years. But the fact remains that in theory the ideal has always been conceded and has never been seriously challenged. People in the West have agreed that theoretically they ought to live according to the teaching of Jesus, even if they never succeeded in doing so. Therefore the Christian ethic has been a place where the minds of men could meet to attempt to resolve their differences and to make their peace with one another.

The most striking thing about our time is the fact that this theoretical obligation to Christian morals and this actual meeting place for minds are being destroyed before our eyes. We are confronted in the dictator and totalitarian states with regimes which frankly disclaim all moral affinity with Christianity. So far from stopping to bother over the question whether Christianity is practicable they go quite unashamedly on to say that they do not think it is even desirable.

They simply do not wish to live after the Christian pattern, even if they could. I do not know that the actual deeds of the present Soviet and Nazi regimes are worse than anything that Christendom has ever known. We might find within the nominal Christendom of the last sixteen hundred years parallels for Jew-baiting, racial persecution, and horrible inquisitorial tortures. What is new is the deliberate cult of the gospel of Antichrist, the repudiation of pity, the faith in falsehoods, the spread of the cult of studied cruelty. This idea derives in our time mainly from the books written a half-century ago by Nietzsche. The cult of Antichrist was not, of course, wholly new with him. It had been foretold by Machiavelli in Italy and Hobbes in England. But they were men born before their time, voices crying in the wilderness. Nietzsche's gospel, however, fell on good soil, the soil of political and economic unrest, and has born fruit a hundredfold in Germany and Russia. According to Rauschning the deliberate aim of the Nazi regime is the destruction of the historic unity of Europe, and therefore a frontal attack on Christian moral ideals which until this latest day have been perhaps the main mode of this unity or means to it.

Meanwhile these prophets and practitioners of a consciously and deliberately unchristian social order are not without warrant for their faith. They draw that faith in the last analysis from what they regard as the strong and cruel processes of nature. Nature is red in tooth and claw; if man as the child of nature, is to run true to form, he must be the same. A recent Gifford Lecturer in Scotland has said that while it may be true that God is our Father, it is even more true that nature is our mother, and if you ask where we get the cruel traits which are so evident in us he can only answer, "from our mother's side." From the first page to the last of his long book he seems to doubt whether any religion, even the Christian religion, can ever make much headway against the lusting, gnawing, fighting instincts of animal man, since man is his mother's child.

That is really the moral problem which the Western world faces. It has many aspects and many answers have been proposed. It is said for example that our picture of the ruthlessness and brutality of nature is overdrawn, that we have heightened the color in the horrors. One school of biologists claims that mutual aid rather than internecine warfare is the basic law of nature, that the universe is probably more like the thirteenth chapter of First Corinthians than we have allowed ourselves to suppose.

Yet all the while the problem presses closer and closer home. Are the democracies and the Christian churches fighting a losing battle because they are attempting to do something which is so essentially unnatural as to be ultimately impossible? Does scientific candor compel us to haul down the flag of all our gentler ideals and surrender to the ape and the tiger

that survives in us all? Are Hitler and Stalin bound to
win because they have at last had the courage to tell
the truth, because the stars in their courses and the
fabric of all things are on their side? Are those of us
who think otherwise the gallant soldiers of a cause
which is already as good as lost? Such is the major
moral problem of our time, which has come out of
holes in the wall, out of revolutionary cellars and
garrets, into the open light of historical day.

There are in this area three possible points of view
and lines of conduct open to you. You may conclude
that you are your mother's son, the child of willful,
wanton, brutal nature and proceed accordingly. Your
heredity is so strong that there is no possibility of your
denying it or altering it, therefore it is the part of
wisdom to accept your destiny. With the poet you will
thank whatever gods that be for

> The primal blessing in the blood. . . .
> The tidal race of lust from shore to shore . . .
> The lewd, perennial, overmastering spell
> That keeps the rolling universe ensphered,
> And life, and all for which life lives to long,
> Wanton and wondrous and for ever well.

If this is your appraisal of your nature there is little
use in further hypocrisies. You had best break with
the traditional conventions and restraints and take the
consequences. You may suffer temporarily by so doing,

but you will be for posterity one of the emancipators. One cannot wholly suppress a perverse admiration for the deliberate immoralists of our day who have the courage of their convictions.

Or you may say, it is true that the processes of nature are cruel and the consequences pitiable, but though I am still lower than the angels I am at least higher than the brutes. I have, with Tennyson, glimpses of a final height where the yelp of the beast will be silenced. The essence of morality is to be found in our capacity to resist and overcome our heritage from the ape and the tiger. This was the position taken by Thomas Huxley in his famous Romanes Lecture, *Evolution and Ethics*, delivered at Oxford nearly fifty years ago—an essay that was a milestone in the history of nineteenth-century thought:

Social progress means a checking of the cosmic process at every step and the substitution for it of another, which may be called the ethical process; the end of which is not the survival of those who may happen to be fittest, but of those who are ethically best. The practice of that which is ethically best—what we call goodness or virtue —involves a course of conduct which, in all respects, is opposed to that which leads to success in the cosmic struggle for existence. In place of ruthless self-assertion it demands self-restraint; in place of thrusting aside or treading down all competitors, it requires that the individual shall not merely respect but help his fellows; its influence is directed, not so much to the survival of the fittest, as to the fitting of as many as possible to survive. It repudiates the gladiatorial theory of existence. . . . Let us understand, once for all, that the ethical progress of society depends, not on imitating the cosmic process, still less in running away from it, but in combating it.[3]

Huxley's position is still reputable and possible. Many earnest persons hold it. It concedes a duality and radical contrast as between the processes of nature and the duty of man. It finds in the resulting moral struggle the meaning and zest of human life, and in such victories as have been won thus far the true reward of life. It is this struggle above all others which keeps the soul alive.

Finally, you may conclude that there is more hidden good in the processes of nature than you at first supposed. Once concede that death is the price which individuals in this world have to pay for the possibility of evolution as a whole and you have made your peace with the one dark fact against which every living thing rebels, because of its innate will to live. You may then debate at leisure the measures of mercy or cruelty which are manifest in nature's devices for achieving the death of one generation for the sake of giving the next generation its chance. We have probably overestimated the degree of cruelty in nature's devices for dealing death. In the main animals which die a natural death seem to do so without any excess of pain. At

[3] T. H. Huxley, *Evolution and Ethics and Other Essays* (New York: D. Appleton and Company, 1914), pp. 81 ff.

least they are spared the horrors of mental anticipation. Nature tends to kill swiftly when she kills; she does not linger over morbid tortures. It is in the human world where there is mental anticipation, where unnatural conditions of life have vastly increased the pain of dying or the tortures which one individual inflicts upon another—it is in the human world rather than in the cosmic process, that this problem takes on its more poignant forms. You cannot "whitewash" nature, as some one has put it, but neither may you invest it with romantic fallacy; you may not read into it all our human joys and sorrows. It may well be that the total pattern for life on this planet is conceived with goodness rather than with evil or indifference, that our world is a stage set by providence rather than by devils. The sterner aspects of nature may be the more obvious; her gracious aspects tend to appear only when we think of her task in the long, and over the millennia of animal evolution. So long as you are in rebellion against the fact of death you will probably quarrel with the processes of nature and history. Once you have made your private peace with the wisdom of death you may begin to see in the totality of things a goodness that was hidden from you at the first.

It may well be, then, that something like Christ's gospel of love, which is the heart of the Christian ethic, is nearer to the deeper truth of nature and history than we are sometimes able to believe. Personally, and without any conscious attempt to tinker with my own mind, I have found my thought moving latterly in this direction. I have found it moving in this direction because the opposite ethic is patently so suicidal. No sane person can suppose that societies conceived and conducted as are contemporary Russia and Germany, can permanently survive. They carry within them the germs of their own dissolution. That dissolution may not be achieved in our time. But that it must come we cannot doubt. A man who lived and worked within the Nazi regime and who has now fled from it as a thing of horror—Rauschning—says,

The destruction of character is the great achievement of National Socialism. The cynicism with which everybody has been willing to justify his capitulation before the terrorist regime bears eloquent witness to the moral disintegration beneath the surface of the "united nation" . . . Five years of the present course have so depreciated every standard that nothing remains with which to build up any better system. If things are allowed to take their course there will remain nothing but an utterly wearied, sceptical, atomized nation, incapable for years to come of any united effort.[4]

Though the end is not yet, that such must be the end is a handwriting on the wall of history, visible to any one who will look twice. It is the patent debase-

[4] Hermann Rauschning, *Germany's Revolution of Destruction* (London: Wm. Heinemann, Ltd., 1939), pp. 100-101.

ment and defeat of all that seems to be intended by
life itself, at the hands of a deliberately and fully conscious anti-Christian ethic, which has led me to believe that the truth of all things must be nearer the
mind and the method of Christ than the more obvious facts suggest. Let us not take cheap and premature
comfort from such a thought. The world has always
known that Armageddons, if and when they come, are
tragically costly affairs, that they may well last longer
than we like, may outlast our day. Our generation may
even now be facing a "thirty years' war," or a "hundred years' war"; there were such wars in the past,
intermittent, sporadic, but never interrupted. What we
need is not the immediate assurance that the mighty
scourge of war may pass speedily away, earnestly as we
may pray for that happy issue; what we need is the
long-range faith that in casting our lot with the Beati-
tudes and the thirteenth chapter of First Corinthians
we are on what must be in the end the winning, not
the losing, side. Remote as the realization of that hope
may be at any given time, this is the Christian faith,
and those of us who profess and call ourselves Christians have no alternative but to hold it in good conscience. Meanwhile if there are times when the whole
problem of the true nature of morality seems an open
question, and when making a moral choice means taking a personal risk, there is sufficient warrant for taking
a Christian risk. The burden of proof today is on men
who make up official Germany and Russia, not on

members of the Society of Friends. The issue comes
to us constantly and imperiously as a daily choice,
determining the motives and ends of our conduct.

"What think ye of Christ," friend? when all's done and
    said,
Like you this Christianity or not?
It may be false, but will you wish it true?
Has it your vote to be so if it can?

Chapter V

GOD

THE FIFTH AND FINAL WORD WHICH WE HAVE PRO-
POSED IN OUR LIST OF SUBJECTS IS THE WORD "GOD."
For religion this is the first and last of all words.

I

The oldest formal creed in the Christian Church is the
Apostles' Creed, so-called not because it was written
by the Apostles, but because the Church in Rome,
which apparently drew up a first draft in the middle
of the second century for use in the baptismal service,
regarded its brief propositions as setting forth in simple
sequence what had been for a century the substance
of the Christian faith. The first article of that Creed is
the majestic affirmation, "I believe in God the Father
Almighty." All that follows is a consequence or corollary of that initial statement.

We have said and heard these words so often that
we tend to forget the bold confidence which first inspired them and the constant trust which has thereafter sustained them. For even at this late date men
are by no means agreed that there is any God at all,
much less a God who is "the Father of our Lord Jesus

Christ." Indeed, there was a sect in the second century, finally declared heretical, which held that the
God revealed in Christ was so unlike any god or gods
of whom men had prior knowledge in nature and history, that they could only say that he was then made
manifest for the first time. For some years it was an
open question whether the God of the Christians
should be recognized as one and the same with God
the Creator of the world, so different were the patent
ways of nature and history from the character of the
God of whom Jesus spoke.

To this day men feel that difficulty. And because
of the felt difficulty of finding Christ's loving Father
in the impersonal immensities of time and space, as
these are now spread before us, many men are de-
terred, and in their own thinking even prohibited, from
saying the first article of the Creed with good conscience. In a letter to a friend, Thomas Huxley puts
the case in blunt form; "I cannot see one shadow or
tittle of evidence that the great unknown underlying
the phenomena of the universe stands to us in the relation of a Father—loves us and cares for us as Christianity asserts." Countless persons, among them numbers of the most intelligent and conscientious of our
fellow citizens, hold substantially that position today.
It is not for us to criticize them or reproach them, but
rather to try to understand them.

Let us realize that in these matters we cannot always
draw a sharp line between those who doubt or deny

and those who affirm. At a meeting in Yale a year or
so ago a prominent Anglican from London, with whom
I was sharing a public discussion, shot an unexpected
question at me. He said, "Has it ever occurred to you
that the Christian religion may not be true?" In all
honesty I had to answer, "Yes, certainly. And I do not
know that I could feel that I really believed it, unless
at times I had doubted it." There is no need for any
man to be ashamed to admit that he has faced this
possibility.

One of the noblest professions of religious faith of
which we have any record is that naked act of self-
dedication attributed to Job, "Though he slay me, yet
will I trust him." Religion finds it hard to go beyond
these words. They are the farthest outpost of faith. Yet
it was this same man, Job, who said in another place,
"Behold I go forward, but he is not there; and backward, but I cannot perceive him. On the left hand
where he doth work, but I cannot behold him: he
hideth himself on the right hand, that I cannot see
him." The prophet Isaiah, the spokesman for a God
who was supposed to reveal himself clearly, says,
"Verily, thou art a God that hidest thyself." This
doctrine of the hidden God—the *Deus Absconditus*—
was fastened upon by Blaise Pascal as the cornerstone
of his theological system: "God being thus hidden,
every religion which does not say that God is hidden
is not the true religion. *Vere tu es Deus absconditus.*

Recognize, then, the truth of every religion in the obscurity of religion."

John Calvin was the father and formulator of most of our Protestant theology. However far we may have gone beyond him, he remains our point of departure. And it is Calvin who writes in his *Institutes*, "The essence of God, indeed, is incomprehensible." Cardinal Newman, at a later time and in a church which supposedly is sure of the substance of its beliefs admits that, "Of all points of faith, the being of a God is, to my own apprehension, encompassed with most difficulty." Testimony to this effect might be multiplied indefinitely. I cite these instances merely to suggest that if at times you have found it hard to believe in God, to imagine what he must be like, to understand his ways in the world, you are not alone with your problem; rather, you are in the company of countless of the world's most earnest thinkers and most holy souls. Let me conclude with a single modern testimony as to this difficulty. It is taken from a sermon that was preached at a great church gathering in 1912 by Dr. Charles Jefferson—preached therefore before the first World War and antedating all the doubts and heart-searchings which followed with the post-war period, only to be revived by the second World War:

The most difficult article in our creed is the first one, "I believe in God." Those who think most know this best. The universe which science has discovered is a vast machine. Its wheels turn inexorably and remorselessly. The winds are pitiless and the stars are cold. Not only is nature indifferent to our cries . . . she shrieks against the Christian creed. History shrieks even louder than nature. It is longer than we supposed; how long no man knows. From the beginning the life of man on earth has been tragedy. The earth has been soaked again and again with blood. Pyramids have been built of human skulls. Empires have risen only to sink in smoke and agony. Races have flourished for a season and then vanished into oblivion. When one stands in the midst of the vast plain of human history, with the tombs of empires and races at his feet, and the past rises before him hideous and gory it is not easy to stand between the vast machine of nature and the vast slaughter house of history and say with a voice that does not falter, "I believe in God the Father Almighty."[1]

We have had in modern America few spokesmen for the Christian religion more confident and full of serene faith than was the writer of these words. His utter candor, in admitting the difficulties of belief in the first article of the Christian Creed, should silence those who pretend that there is no problem here and should encourage us in those hours when we feel the force of the problem, with the reassurance that we are not without comrades in the company of good men.

One of my friends insists that many, if not most, of the difficulties of religion in our times arise from the

[1] Report of the National Council of Congregational Churches, meeting at Kansas City, Mo., 1912.

modern attempt to make knowledge do duty for faith. That is signally true in the case of the first article of the Creed. The astronomer tells us that he has swept the heavens with his telescope and has found no God. Other scientists, restricting themselves to findings reached with the help of their apparatus, have to say the same thing; no single technique has found God, no known system of weights and measures has demonstrated him. If we must confine our thoughts to what we know scientifically we shall have to reconcile ourselves to ignorance of God, in the terms of that kind of knowledge which is had by the measurements of science.

Meanwhile the restless, eager, ardent mind of man is curiously unwilling and unable to keep within these bounds. As we have already said, you cannot stop men asking why we are here and what it all means. Pascal has put our lot in memorable words:

When I consider the short duration of my life, swallowed up in eternity before and after, the small place which I fill, or even can see, engulfed in the immensity of spaces whereof I know nothing, and which know nothing of me, I am terrified, and wonder that I am here rather than there, for there is no reason why here rather than there, or now rather than then. Who has set me here? By whose order and design have this place and time been destined for me? . . . The eternal silence of these infinite spaces terrifies me.

It has always seemed to me little short of miracle that Pascal, who lived and wrote in the middle of the seventeenth century, three hundred years ago, should have anticipated so accurately what has become the somber mood of the modern mind as it looks out upon the ever-expanding universe. We have been the victims of a barrage of terrific facts which are the instruments of what some one has called a process of "astronomical intimidation." Our case has been poignantly put by more than one spokesman, seldom better than by Father Tyrrell in his commentary on the beginning of the Lord's Prayer, "Our Father who art in heaven":

If astronomy has in some ways enlarged, it has also impoverished, our notion of the heavens. It has given us quantitative mysteries in exchange for qualitative; it has made heaven homogeneous with earth. The once mysterious planets, and the sun itself, are but material orbs like our own; and as the mind travels endlessly into space it meets only with more orbs and systems of orbs in their millions, an infinite monotony of matter and motion, but never does it strike against some boundary wall of the universe, beyond which God keeps an eternal Sabbath in a new order of existence, a mysterious world which eye has not seen, nor ear heard, nor heart conceived. The heaven that lay behind the blue curtain of the sky, whence by night God hung out His silver lamps to shine upon the earth, was a far deeper symbol of the eternal home than the cold, shelterless deserts of astronomical space.[2]

[2] George Tyrrell, *Lex Credendi* (New York: Longmans, Green and Company, 1906), pp. 109-10.

A recent writer has said that "all the forces which
play upon us conspire to make belief in God difficult.
In the old world every one believed in God: that is perhaps the most signal difference between ancient and
modern history." The result of this astronomical intimidation which Tyrrell describes with such truth-
fulness, of the play of forces upon the modern mind
of which the other writer speaks, is to numb us. Countless men, going about their daily, useful work in the
world, put on a bold front of cheerfulness, but this
good face which they turn to their fellow men hides a
gray suspicion that human life in its totality has no
meaning. Single words in our experience may make
sense, but the sentences break down, the paragraphs
are inconclusive, and the whole story comes to nothing
in the end. I should rate this dull dread that life is
meaningless as being the most characteristic form of
religious doubt in our time.

For those who believe unquestioningly in what is
called revealed religion there is no serious problem
here. That any God, who is to be a partner in the religious relationship as we have described it, must reveal
himself, goes without saying. He must have given indi-
cations of his presence, and intimations of his nature
and character. The initial act of religion must be God's
not ours; "We love him because he first loved us."
There have been, it is true, philosophies which assumed that there was some kind of a God at the heart
or at the boundaries of things, but a God who said

nothing and did nothing, who was the eternal object of man's seeking, but who gave no response to the perennial human quest for him. These systems hardly came alive as religions to touch man's heart. The unresponsive deities whom the human mind has conceived lose their plausibility and vanish into thin air, and the perpetually frustrated human suitor finally draws from his experience the only possible inference —there is no God. The idea of religion requires confidence in the possibility and indeed the reality of some actual transaction between God and man. If you think no God hears your prayers you will finally give up saying your prayers; you cannot keep them up indefinitely once you suspect that they are nothing more than autosuggestion.

But although we hold that the initial conception of religion requires the idea of a divine self-revelation, we have to admit that such revelation has never been so plain and unequivocal that it has yielded self-evident truths which all men must accept as a matter of course. The very fact that vast numbers of men still do not believe in the existence of God, and that those who do believe are often invaded by doubt, should satisfy us that whatever the nature of a revealed religion may be, it is not of a kind which proves its case mechanically and universally.

Within religions which hold to the idea of a divine revelation, each religion has therefore had to fashion its own canons for testing and validating the content of revelation. All historic religions claim to be the heirs of divine revelations made to them in the past. So, also, living men claim today to be the chosen recipients or vessels of revelations made to them privately in the present. How are we to know that these claims are true? That has been, and still is, a problem with which religion has wrestled from time immemorial. The particular devices which a church sets up to accredit a supposed revelation may be satisfactory to those within the fold, but they carry no proof to persons outside. Both Kaiser Wilhelm II and Hitler have talked with the utmost confidence about God's will for the German people and its patent destiny under the divine favor. Each of these men has undoubtedly been sincere. That is the tragedy of it. Furthermore they have succeeded in convincing a vast number of their fellow Germans as well as themselves. But the rest of us are unconvinced. Yet how prove that they are wrong? All men tend, in these matters, to argue in closed circles, and the proofs which we offer of the reality of the revelation we claim to have received are themselves geared in advance to guarantee that proof. Calvin asks, "How am I to know that the Bible is true?" He answers his own question by saying, "Because of the witness of the Spirit within me to its truth." "But," he then asks, "how am I to know that the Spirit which bears witness in me is the Holy Spirit of God, and not some spirit of error and delusion?" This is a very real question, and all prophets, saints, mystics and theologians have had to reckon with the possibility that the witnessing spirit within them may be a lying spirit. So Calvin goes on to answer his question about the nature of the spirit within him by concluding, "I am to be certain that the Spirit within me is the Spirit of God and of truth, rather than of error, because of its conformity to the letter of the Bible." He has come back where he started, and has traveled inside a closed circle. To do him justice he admits that his argument may seem circular, and then passes on to another subject.

Most proofs of revelation tend to be of this sort. They are buttresses for a faith we intend to hold in any case, for beliefs which we will or wish to believe, rather than independent vindications of revelation. So far as I can find, religion has only one convincing proof of supposed revealed truths, "By their fruits ye shall know them." Only the consequences in character of an idea set to work as a dominant consideration in the mind of a man or a society can discover, after the passage of time, the truth or error of that idea. This is what Professor Hocking has called the test of "negative pragmatism." Not, "if it works, it is true"; rather, "If it is true, it will work." With the proviso that it may take a truth of religion a longer rather than a shorter time to prove its efficacy.

Of the more sophisticated proofs of revelation Browning once said with picturesque accuracy,

Each method abundantly convincing
    To those already convinced;
But scarce to be swallowed without wincing
    By the not as yet convinced.

II

I have no mind here to try to fortify the faith of those who are already fully convinced of the truth of a revelation they have accepted or received. Such persons need no help. But I am concerned for those who remain unconvinced by such proofs, and yet who are quite willing to admit that there may be a God and that he has revealed himself to us.

No serious theology has ever put such persons religiously out of bounds. For very few thinkers have claimed that revealed religion is the only religion accessible to us; they hold, rather, that the particular revelations in which they believe confirm and carry forward some form of religion less explicit than that at which they have finally arrived. In particular the classical Christian theologians, without denying the distinctive revelation which our religion finds in the life and work of Christ, have admitted the existence of a general capacity for religion in all men. So, for example, Calvin says, "We hold it to be beyond dispute that there exists in the human mind, and indeed by natural instinct, some sense of Deity. . . . This sense of Deity is inscribed on every heart. . . . This is not a doctrine which is first learned at school, but one as to which every man is, from the womb, his own master; one which nature herself allows no individual to forget." It is with this innate and natural bent or capacity for religion that I am here and now concerned.

There are various classical arguments for the existence of God and they bear formidable names; there are the cosmological and teleological arguments, which stress on the one hand the need of finding some point of departure for creation and on the other hand the need of demonstrating a moral purpose in the world and some point of ethical arrival at history's end. There is also the famous ontological argument which says that the very fact that we have the idea of God suggests that there must be a reality which corresponds to that idea, otherwise how did we get the idea? The first two of these arguments have always seemed to me less interesting than the third. As for the so-called cosmological argument, that has been in the past the one most often in men's minds. Here is the world, there are the stars; it is all very mysterious and must have come from something at some time. The analogy of human experience would suggest that some one must have made it; hence the doctrine of a creator God. The idea is so obvious as to be almost inevitable. But it has no answer to the further question which has occurred to many an inconveniently persistent child, "Who made God?" Furthermore, in the terms of modern thought, God the creator, instead of finishing his work in six days some six thousand years ago, is now infinitely removed from us in time and space. It is hard to imagine what lies at the boundary of the preposterous light years with which today we are confronted. The thought of God creating the heavens and the earth is not as easy to come by as it was when the universe was a smaller affair.

Hence many men have turned their minds in the other direction and have preached to us a God who is to be sought and found at the end of the road of history, particularly as that road is conceived of as a highway for the human conscience journeying toward a realization of its moral ideals. When we reach our ideals, they say, then we shall find not barren and impersonal theories come true, but some personal being who has all the time been foreshadowed in those ideals in advance of our struggles and has given them their reality for us. Whatever we may think about God as the beginning of life we may, on this count, think of him as the end of life. So construed the end of the moral struggle is to be a finding and falling in love with God, as when Synge's Playboy says to Pegeen, "It's miracles, and that's the truth. Me there toiling a long while, and walking a long way, not knowing at all that I was drawing all times nearer to this holy day." But this conception of God as a goal of life is in some ways open to the same objection which can be raised to the elder doctrine of God the creator of all things; we may suspect that it is merely a name which we give to an end of things we cannot foresee, and which certainly we shall not reach for untold millennia of years.

Religion has always required some conception of God more immediate than all this. You cannot sustain it permanently on the inconclusive, indeterminate mood which Clough wrote into four familiar lines,

> Where lies the land to which the ship would go?
> Far, far ahead is all her seamen know.
> And where the land she journeys from? Away,
> Far, far behind is all that they can say.

Therefore, the third of the classical arguments for God is the most likely to give us the lead which we seek. Not perhaps in its literal form, that the fact we have an idea of God requires a reality to match the idea— but rather that our human thoughtfulness is not a thing by itself without any parallel in the rest of the universe.

What Wordsworth calls "man's unconquerable mind" is the most impressive thing we know here and now. We follow its gradual emergence from its animal beginnings, we trace its tremendous acceleration since the dawn of civilization, we record its almost incredible achievements in the last hurrying century of science. "Wisdom," says *Ecclesiasticus*, "has rained down skill." That downpour has now become a veritable cloudburst, and we cannot today manage the torrents let loose upon the world by our technical skills, which

have so far outrun our moral power to employ them
to man's help rather than his hurt. Yet this ceaseless
thinking, thinking, thinking, goes on, an insatiable
intellectual restlessness and curiosity sharpened by the
purposes which direct it. Under the caption of this
thoughtfulness come all men's enduring affections,
since his love is more than lust. Here too, are his
works of art, intricate and utterly lovely, the glass of
his old cathedrals and the movements of his symphonies. Shot through all heedless instincts and wayward actions is this incessant thoughtfulness, so that
the statue of Rodin's "Thinker" is far more faithful
to the human fact than any unbowed figure ever
could be.

Now the question which I always find that I am
asking myself is this, Does all this thinking go on
without any real parallel or kinship in the universe
around? The mind of man finds in his world a realm
of law. The steady mastery of its laws makes his world
not merely manageable, but increasingly intelligible.
Does the mind of man impute to the natural order
something that is not there? If the universe is nothing
more than an accidental collocation of atoms, it seems
strange that the sum of these countless accidents all
along the line should be amenable to reasonable interpretation, if they themselves are chaotic and irrational.
We say, and say properly that we find the laws of
nature, but do we make them? If we find them, are
they not there in the first instance to be found? And

if they are there waiting to be found, how did they come there?

I once put the problem this way to a friend who is by nature skeptical in these matters, "If the human race were to be wiped off this planet tonight by the often prophesied collision with some wandering star, and if a similar catastrophe were to overtake other planets where there may be other human beings like ourselves—let us say, Mars—would the process which we know as thinking have ceased utterly in the universe?" And he said, "No, I don't really believe that it would. Man's mind cannot be the last wild accident in the sum of the cosmic chances. It must be in some way part of the whole order of things." "Well," I said, "then you have all that I ask at the outset for belief in a God."

The terms which we use as tentative descriptions of God are figures of speech. Let us not make the mistake of thinking of them as definitions. Such were the older metaphors, King, Lord, Sovereign. Such also is the characteristic Christian term, Father; it is at the best a metaphor, nothing more. Meanwhile, I often find my mind turning to Wordsworth's ascription to God, "Thou, who art an eternity of thought." That is, to my mind, not merely a suggestive, but a credible phrase.

Of course it is true that the processes of nature do not always seem thoughtful, at least thoughtful of us. Nature, as we meet her in her wayward seasons and wanton ways, often seems irrational if not actually insane in the terms of her hurricanes, her blizzards, her volcanic outbursts. Let us not forget that we sometimes invite her more savage attacks upon us by tempting her. We skate on her thin ice with the recklessness of youth. If we choose to live on the slopes of Vesuvius we must accept the risks of that locale, for Vesuvius has posted warning notice on her human neighbors with streams of hardened lava. If you live in Florida you cannot ignore the risk of a hurricane, and if you build your home in California you must reckon with the chance of earthquakes. Of the day and the hour no man knoweth; but man does know what is implied by the climate of the Caribbean and the geologic faults along the Pacific coast line. The immediate irrationality of a single unwelcome event does not dispel our more sober knowledge of the rationale of nature in her longer processes. The thoughts graven into nature are long, long thoughts, they belong to an "eternity of thought." Some long-range reliability in the total scheme of things, accessible to our human understanding, seems to be implied by the facts themselves.

If it is difficult for us to believe in this probability it is equally difficult to accept the alternative, for the alternative does not make sense. The near-at-hand occasions for religious doubts are so obvious that they need not be labored. We have all felt them. But the path of studied skepticism, if followed to its conclusion,

ends in a cul-de-sac that asks even greater credulity
of us than is required by a positive faith. There is, for
example, in Camille Flammarion's *Astronomie Popu-
laire*, a harrowing picture of the end of life on this
planet, which is presumably to be also the extinction
of thought in the universe:

Life and human activity will insensibly be shut up
within the tropical zones. Saint Petersburg, Berlin, London, Paris, Vienna, Constantinople, Rome, will succes-
sively sink to sleep under their eternal cerements. During
many centuries, equatorial humanity will undertake vain
arctic expeditions to rediscover under the ice the sites of
Paris, Bordeaux, of Lyons, of Marseilles. The seashores
will have changed and the map of the earth will be trans-
formed. No longer will man live—no longer will he breathe
—except in the equatorial zone, down to the day when the
last tribe, already expiring in cold and hunger, shall camp
on the shores of the last sea in the rays of a pale sun which
will henceforward illumine an earth that is only a wandering tomb, turning around a useless light and a barren
heat. Surprised by the cold, the last human family has
been touched by the finger of death, and soon their bones
will be buried under the shroud of eternal ice. The historian of nature would then be able to write:—"Here lies
the entire humanity of a world which has lived! Here lie
all the dreams of ambition, all the conquests of military
glory, all the resounding affairs of finance, all the systems
of an imperfect science, and also all the oaths of mortals'
love! Here lie all the beauties of earth!—But no mortuary

stone will mark the spot where the poor planet shall have
rendered its last sight!"[3]

As one of my friends, to whom I was once reading
this passage, said, "That certainly is a depressing
thought, but it will be after our time!" Mercifully this
is so. But as I have already suggested, the long-range
view of doubt really does not make doubt more toler-
able, to say nothing of its being more attractive.
Whether we are attracted or not by such a prophecy
as Flammarion has given us—and some such conclusion to the story of life on this planet seems inevitable
—is beside the mark. It will happen, even though we
do not desire it. The real question is, does this sentence
of death for the mind of man seem more probable than
its religious opposite? I can only say that I find it
harder to believe Flammarion than, let us say, the
fourteenth Chapter of John with its assurance, "In
my father's house are many mansions." It seems to
me more likely than otherwise that there is some permanent part and place in the totality of things for
what we know as human thought, with all the affections and the purposes which it embraces. To believe
that "man's unconquerable mind" is an isolated accident, without counterpart elsewhere in the scheme of
things, and destined to come to nothing at the last,
requires of me a credulity even greater than that asked
by faith in God. I can only conclude that man's think-

[3] Henry Adams, The Degradation of the Democratic Dogma (New
York: The Macmillan Company, 1919), pp. 182-3.

ing is a process akin to something going on throughout time and space, and that our attempts to achieve some correspondence to this "eternity of thought" and permanent share in it is the basis of religion. I must believe that in some such terms there is a God.

III

I come now to two or three of the familiar problems which attend that faith, particularly in the forms in which we most often meet it in the Christian religion.

Critics of religion are accustomed to indict it and then dismiss it on the ground that all our thinking about these mysterious matters is "anthropomorphic," i.e., done in the terms of human experience. Of that fact there is no doubt; it has been recognized from the first. Thus Xenophanes, a Greek thinker of the sixth century B.C., says in a classic passage,

Mortals fancy gods are born, and wear clothes, and have voice and form like themselves.

If oxens and lions had hands and could paint with their hands, and fashion images, as men do, they would make the pictures and images of their gods in their own likeness; horses would make them like horses, oxen like oxen.

Ethiopians make their gods black and snub-nosed; Thracians give theirs blue eyes and red hair.

No one questions the truth of the statement. Indeed the most sensitive religious natures have always been

aware of the fact and anxious to save the anthropomorphism of their faith from its more obvious abuses.
They have known that God is something more and
other than a transcript, infinitely enlarged, of any
given man or group of men. God is not German or
English or American, difficult though it is for nationals
to admit the fact of a difference, and natural as it is
for them to affirm the identity. "Thou thoughtest that
I was altogether such an one as thyself," says God in
the Bible, and the statement carries with it the implied
rebuke.

Nevertheless, you cannot wholly dispense with anthropomorphism in your thought of God, save at the
cost of giving up thinking of him altogether, and
labeling him the "transcendent X," or as Mr. Wells
does, the "Veiled Being." That is because you cannot
think any other way than anthropomorphically, in the
terms of human experience. Modern physics, as I
understand it, is at great pains to say that its thinking
is frankly anthropomorphic. It does not profess that
its patterns correspond to the nature of the physical
universe. It does say that these patterns, which represent processes of our human minds, do give us some
understanding of what is happening, and how it happens. If you are to deny yourself all anthropomorphic
thinking, you will have to give up thinking altogether,
since thinking has to be done for better or for worse
with the brains we have and in the terms of our own
life. To refuse to think thus would be very like refusing

to ride in a Ford, because it isn't a Lincoln. There are fastidious persons who demand a Lincoln or nothing, but most of us are quite willing to get on with the Ford which we actually have. So it is with our mental outfit. From the ideal standpoint it may be inadequate, but it "goes," and therefore we do well to trust it as far as it will carry us, rather than to quarrel with it at the start and get nowhere whatsoever. I am quite willing therefore to admit the strain of anthropomorphism in man's thought of God, and to admit also the need of constant self-criticism and self-correction in any given idea of God. But I do not see how, if you are to think of God at all, you can think in any other way, since the apparatus for all thought is human, and every idea we have is necessarily anthropomorphic.

Meanwhile, in our world of human experiences, most of us would agree that of all that matters to us, persons matter most. There is a verse in the Old Testament which says, "Give me the persons, and take the goods to thyself." Faced with a choice between the persons and things, most of us would stand with that verse. It follows naturally, then, that we ascribe to God the highest designation and value which we know— personality. Let us realize, however, that although we know persons, we have no single clear definition of personality. And we do not solve the problem of what constitutes human personality by appealing to the idea of divine personality. Our idea of personality is identified with single individuals—and we have little understanding of what personality may be apart from individuality. We get now and then an intimation of some personal life which is more than individual in the emotions and the acts of a crowd fused for the moment into a whole, but these intimations are fugitive and hard to analyze. In the meantime the plain fact that we know persons as individuals does create a problem for our thought of God, for plainly God is not just one more individual like ourselves. When orthodox theology suffers its doctrine of the three persons of the Trinity to be construed as denoting three quite distinct individuals, as we know individuality, it has ceased to affirm belief in one God and becomes faith in three gods. This is polytheism rather than monotheism. Whatever the doctrine of the Trinity may mean it ought not to be a denial of monotheism.

But having said so much as to the limitations of the idea of personality as applied to God, the stubborn fact remains that it is only in the terms of personal relationships that we can think of religion. And from the possible permutations and combinations of our human relationships Christianity has fastened upon that of Father and son as best intimating its idea. Let us admit that this is a metaphor and not a definition. When the New Testament writer says, "Beloved, now are we the sons of God, and it doth not yet appear what we shall be," he uses the metaphor in entire good faith, but in the added words admits its possible inadequacy. The metaphor does not exhaust the idea.

Nevertheless, if we are to take any figure of speech whatsoever from human life, the Father-son metaphor is singularly appropriate. As Phillips Brooks has said,

In all human uses, the idea of fatherhood comes nearer to being a religious idea than that of any other human relationship. . . . It includes the notions of a common nature between the Father and the son, of a spontaneous affection of the Father, of an essential obligation of the son, and of a possibility of a son's unlimited growth into the Father's likeness. . . . (Jesus) always treats the truth of Fatherhood as the best children of the best earthly fathers treat it, not ignorant of the elemental truths of which it is composed, but best satisfied to let it rest in its own unity, as if any analysis must disturb its beauty and its power.

If we look elsewhere in the world of human relationships for some other metaphor to describe the religious life, the relationship which has most often been employed is that of husband and wife. This imagery is quite familiar in the non-Christian religions, and has indeed crept into Christian piety through hymns and mystical writings as the thought of the soul, or of the church, as the bride of Christ. There is no warrant in the teaching of Jesus for this sexual symbolism, and most of us are aware of the abuses to which it is liable. The appearance of what may be called the erotic motif in religion is apt to be the prelude to excessive sentimentalism, and in more extreme cases to licentiousness. The fact of sex, which bulks so large in modern thought, receives little attention in the Gospels. In heaven, so the Gospel saying runs, there will be neither marrying nor giving in marriage. The Gospels are not severely ascetic in their attitude toward sex, as certain types of later Christianity tended to become; they are, perhaps, merely indifferent to it. But as against much religious mythology elsewhere there is from their first page to the last page a chastity of which we are all aware.

Now it is to be said for the Father-son metaphor, that, while preserving the elements of likeness and unlikeness as between God and man which the idea of religion requires, it stands quite clear of the sentimentalism to which the husband-wife metaphor is always liable, or to the more complex emotions which sometimes attend the mother-son, father-daughter relationships. We are so familiar with the doctrine of the Fatherhood of God and the thought of our own sonship to him, that we forget the essential dignity and strength and wholesome connotation of this metaphor as against other metaphors drawn from our more intimate human relationships.

The doctrine of the Fatherhood of God needs, however, in twentieth-century America safeguarding and reinterpretation at one vital point. The American father is generally conceived of as a tolerant and convenient person to whom one turns as a matter of course for whatever happens to be needed at the moment.

He is seldom spoken of, as in England, as "the gov-
ernor." Indeed the American father is encouraged to
be the "pal" of his son and to try to accommodate
himself to the son. The old idea of parental authority
is very much out of fashion. Now in all these respects
the American father is not the counterpart of the
father in a Jewish home of two thousand years ago.
The Wisdom literature of Israel insists constantly that
the father is the center of values in the home, that
whatever worth attaches to the son is derived from
the father. The whole movement of reference in the
family was from son to father, rather than father to
son. The basic obligation of the son was that of respect and filial duty, his rights and privileges were a
secondary matter. There was, therefore, in the world
which furnished Jesus with his metaphor more of the
idea of divine sovereignty than we realize, particularly
if we draw upon the contemporary family for the
nature of the father-son relationship. Jesus takes it for
granted that God will provide—"your Father knoweth
that ye have need of all these things." God's concern
and care for us is assumed as an axiom, and is not
labored. The more sober teaching of the Gospels
stresses the devotion and duty which, as his sons, we
owe to God. Unless the doctrine of the Fatherhood of
God is to become a blank check for a new kind of
magic, a check to be filled in by ourselves for whatever amount we choose and drawn on an infinite
benevolence, that doctrine needs to recover the refer-

ence of filial duty which first attached to it. God is something more than an endlessly good-natured parent who can be trusted to pay our bad bills!

Once we have seen the doctrine of the Fatherhood of God in something like its original perspective, two or three age-old problems appear. Since these problems must already have arisen in your minds I propose at least to enter them here. Each one of them has been the occasion for a vast literature, and it may be little short of impertinence to cite them so briefly. But I am concerned that we should not seem to deny their stubborn survival in the common mind, and I shall hazard two or three suggestions, as my own tentative answers—not as being in any way sufficient, since no such answer, nor the sum of them, has ever sufficed to quiet all our perplexities—but merely as an indication of certain considerations which seem to me to throw some light on these matters.

I said a few moments ago, that confidence in God's care for each one of his children was an axiom in the thought of Jesus. But many moderns have the greatest difficulty in admitting that axiom. Of all the sayings in the Gospels that about the falling sparrow seems to them the hardest to believe. It was the fashion a generation or so ago to agree that something in the scheme of things does seem to be careful of the species as a whole, but seems to be correspondingly careless of the individual. We have recently read in the papers that the Russian generals directing the Soviet attack on

Finland have been absolutely indifferent as to losses in the ranks. To many persons nature and history, even God himself, seem to display precisely this wanton carelessness of the human individual. The common soldier in the ranks of history does not seem to count for much, as long as the campaign is won. It is only fair to say that not all generals are like those Russians. We are told that, after the Civil War, General Grant was haunted by the suspicion that in some engagements he had perhaps sacrificed his men unnecessarily. So again, the inertia of the first six months of the present "queer" war was due, at least on the Allied side, if widespread reports are to be trusted, to the determination not to throw a single human life needlessly away. Even after the fight is on, the apparatus of modern states cuts both ways, and the healing ministries of surgery and medicine are intent to save with the left hand that single life which the right hand of war is throwing so wantonly away. We are strangely equivocal at this point. The techniques for caring for individuals in the modern world may not be ignored or disparaged. Therefore, analogies from human life do not leave you helpless and hopeless at this crucial point. The evidence is not all of a kind, and you may find intimations of God's ways with men quite as fairly in the person of a surgeon in a base hospital as in the person of the Soviet general.

Once again, since our thought of God is determined, as I have already indicated, by the forms of our human experience and by the habitual manner of our thinking, part of our difficulty in believing that God cares for individuals should probably be charged against the predominantly scientific habits of the modern mind. Science is not interested in individual facts for their own sake; it is interested in them only as data which can be used to yield general laws. Our passion for such abstractions is so great that all our human relations are infected by it. We think of our fellow men as falling into cases, classes, races, sects and the like. We attach a series of these abstract labels to any given individual, then add them up and get what we think is a true account of him. By this method we undoubtedly do learn a good deal about men in general, but the vivid concrete truth of the single individual always slips through the meshes of this net of abstractions.

There is, of course, an entirely different way of looking at facts—the artist's way. The artist is concerned only with the concrete individual fact, in and for itself. He looks at a rose, or a sunset, or a tree, or a human face, and tries to see into it. He shuts out everything else, and in particular does not try to abstract it in any way. When he feels he has seen into it, he writes a poem about it, or paints a picture. I do not think, therefore, that artists would ever have any great difficulty, if they believed in a God at all, in believing in a God who cares for individuals—since such care is the mental manner of their whole life. I suggest, therefore, that we get some help at this point by correcting our too common thought of God as the infinite scientist by thought of God as the divine artist.

In so far as we succeed in conceiving of a loving God who cares for individuals we create for ourselves a further problem. How are we to reconcile the goodness of God with the omnipotence of God? We noticed in our opening lecture that primitive man first became aware of the idea of God through his experience of powers more than human and not amenable to human control, in the world around. In some form or other that idea has always persisted, even though the "power" is eventually invested with moral attributes. Theoretically this divine power is omnipotent. But if God is all-powerful, how can he, if he is also good, suffer so much evil in his world? It is only when stern personal experience gets you on the rack and turns the thumbscrews of its perplexity down upon your mind and heart that you feel the full force of this old problem.

Personally I think the only answer to the problem is this, there must be things which God cannot do, or perhaps is prevented from doing by his own prior choices and acts. In any case, if you have to choose between the omnipotence of God and the goodness of God, you will be religiously more nearly right if you cast your lot with the goodness and let the omnipotence take the consequences. At this late date a religion which celebrates power only, and ignores goodness, cannot satisfy the minds of men, let alone their common decent conscience. Indeed there have grown up many religions which are interested solely in saving men from evil into goodness and care little or nothing for the vindication of some elemental omnipotence in the universe. Within Christianity itself, this distinction is often met, and the plain Christian today is far more concerned for what Whittier called the "Eternal Goodness" than for the divine omnipotence. If, then, you are caught on the horns of this dilemma and can escape only by sacrificing one idea or the other, I should, if I were you, let the dogma of God's omnipotence go for the sake of retaining your confidence in his goodness. It is, perhaps worth remembering that it was said of Jesus in a certain situation, that, "He could do there no mighty works." Those who hold the extreme orthodox and fundamentalist position that Jesus was Deity itself, can draw from these words only one conclusion, there are some things that God cannot do. This, certainly, is an inference which every ethical religion will draw from nature and history, unless it is prepared to be a house divided against itself.

Hence the doctrine of a limited or finite God has been much the fashion in recent years. Let us remember that this idea of a limited God springs not from a loss of religious faith, but is prompted by that kind of faith which is concerned above all else to defend the principle of goodness in things. Since this principle does not seem to be plainly coextensive with the universe as a whole, many men of quick conscience have accepted the consequence of their logic and have admitted that for them God must be a limited being; if he is no longer omnipotent he is at least the will to righteousness fighting eternally against all that is dark and evil in the world. Those of us who are still unable to think of God as being merely the personification of the human will to righteousness in history, struggling to vindicate itself in the face of a hostile universe, would say rather, that having made this world as it is, there are certain things God has denied himself doing thereafter. He must stand by his own acts and his own laws, and is to that extent self-limited. His choices in creation are themselves limitations of his primeval omnipotence.

IV

If we decide, therefore, to cast our religious lot with the goodness of God rather than his omnipotence, we are then confronted at once by the most stubborn of all the problems known to religion, the problem of evil. Phillips Brooks once said that if a man were to come to him saying, "Lo! I will now read you the problem of evil," he would close his ears to the offer. Nothing is so out of place in our thinking as cheap and easy answers to the problem of evil. It is the ultimate mystery in human experience.

But unless we are to stop thinking about the matter

altogether—and this is precisely what we are unable to do in spite of all heroic resolutions to do just that —we must fall back once more upon human analogies. I have already suggested that so far as the world of organic nature is concerned the problem of evil comes down to the final fact of death. Unless you think that every living thing ought to be physically immortal you have to admit the necessity of the death of individuals as the means of evolution and the price of progress. I have further suggested that, on the whole, nature as executioner, if left to herself, tends to do a businesslike job. Not that it is ever pleasant to watch her at this task. I should not like to be a witness at an execution in a state's prison. So I have not liked the moments when I have seen nature at her executioner's work; a terrier killing a rat, a hawk pouncing on a field mouse, a snake swallowing a frog, a spider enmeshing a fly. Few of us are soon and easily persuaded to "whitewash nature," as some one has put it.

Meanwhile, the problem takes on more serious forms when we meet it as "man's inhumanity to man." If God is good, why does he let the Russians kill the Finns and wipe out the decent life of that gallant country? Or why does he condemn so many who are near and known to us to the grim process of dying by inches of painful diseases.

I can only hint at what seems to me to be the one gleam of light on this dark mystery. If man's freedom is real, then he must pay the price for that freedom.

This is often a heavy price. It is a price which is paid by the race as a whole over its long life, and at any given moment the payment asked of the single individual, who may be tragically ignorant or wholly innocent, is unjust. We shall get onto more solid ground in this matter, if we admit that so far as his physical fortunes in this world are concerned—his health, wealth, and long life—many a single individual gets rank injustice in this life. He frequently cries out that this is so. Why not grant him the warrant for his bitter complaint? But this injustice is the cost we pay one by one for being members of humanity as a whole, not isolated, self-sufficient, self-explanatory individuals. The web of life is woven of good fortune and of ill fortune. Individuals are variously involved in the pattern. If there is, for one person, a bitter problem of evil, there is from any theoretical standpoint for another person an equally inscrutable problem of good. Is it because you and I are virtuous persons that we are here in comfort and security, rather than lying as grotesque and frozen corpses on the Karelian Isthmus? Father Tyrrell once said that he believed in the general providence of God, but found it harder to believe in special providences. It is, I think, not impossible to reconcile the larger framework within which human life is set with faith in the general providence of God. Your faith in the goodness of God is shaken only when you begin to ask that exceptions to the general rule be made in your private behalf. It takes a good deal of unselfishness and moral maturity to be willing to agree that the wider and longer purposes of a divine providence are best served if exceptions are not made for importunate individuals.

Meanwhile, an increasing number of us, at this stage of history, have begun to suspect that many of the miseries from which we suffer, at least in their most poignant and cruel forms, are of our own human devising. They are the tragic consequence of an abuse of human freedom. If our freedom is, as most of us believe it is, genuine, then that freedom carries with it the peril that free men may hurt themselves terribly. Such is the price of freedom, and apparently you cannot have what one of the books of the New Testament calls a "goodness which is of free will, and not of necessity," without running the risk of those evils which are also the consequence of freedom rather than necessity.

During all the years of the first World War one was constantly hearing the question, "Why has God let this happen? If he is good, why doesn't he stop it?" I should like to enter here a single pertinent observation. Since the beginning of the second World War I have never heard that question asked. We realize only too well, and with bitterness, that the present tragic facts are our own fault. They are the direct result of the vengefulness, the hatreds, the fear, the stupidity, and the sheer laziness of ourselves and our contemporaries. We have no one but ourselves to thank or blame for the clouds in history which have now returned again after the rain. We have brought the second World War on our own heads. Our liberties are real, our freedom of opportunity to make a better world was in 1918 unlimited. But we were too angry, too unforgiving, perhaps too tired to rise to the occasion. We are under no necessity to charge this latest revival of man's inhumanity to man against God. We have grown up in the last twenty years a little nearer the moral majesty of Lincoln's Second Inaugural, and find no cause in the grim present fact to challenge either the justice or the goodness of God—that God whose judgments in the history of a nation as a whole are true and righteous altogether.

I have dealt in this lecture with the idea of God as it exists in what is usually called the area of natural religion, I have not attempted to deal with any particular form of revealed religion. For most of us that will mean the Christian religion. If we profess and call ourselves Christians we have as Christians our particular reasons for believing in such revelations as to the nature and character of God as have come to the world through Christ. I would point out that in the case of this revealed religion, as in the case of all such religions, the proofs of revelation satisfy those who are already believers, but apparently do not carry final and compelling conviction to persons outside. It is only occasionally, for example, that a Jew is converted to Christianity. And all around us are countless men making no profession of religion, and even indifferent to religion, to whom our reasons for being Christians are either not persuasive or not convincing.

But this is a Christian college and I am speaking to you as a Christian minister, and I should be recreant to my trust if I did not witness briefly to what is our common faith. We believe that the glory of God is seen in the face of Jesus Christ, that he that hath seen the Son hath seen the Father. In our moments of perplexity and distress we say, "Lord, to whom shall we go, thou hast the words of eternal life." We may be right, we may be wrong; this is our faith.

There is for us as Christians one persistent question with which theology has long been familiar. Do we think that the Christian revelation renders all other supposed revelations meaningless, if not actually false? Or do we think that the Christian revelation brings to maturity all insights into religion, all struggles after goodness, all intimations of God, wherever and however had?

The Christian Church in the middle of the second century was faced by this issue. There arose at that time a group of men who said that the God whom Christ revealed was then made known for the first time, that he had no connection with the God of the Old Testament or the God whom the religious philosophies of the classical world had seen in their speculative visions. The gods of Moses and Isaiah, of Plato and Aristotle were declared to be false gods. The only true God was the God whom Christ had made known, of whom the Jewish world beforetimes had known nothing, and of whom the wider Greek and Roman world around knew nothing. Some sense of the newness of Christianity was so strong upon these men that they made a good case for themselves and their interpretation of Christianity. The Church had to decide whether they were right or wrong. It decided that they were wrong and declared therefore that they were heretics. It said that the God who created the world, gave the law to Moses, and inspired the prophets, was also the Father of our Lord Jesus Christ. It went further and said that the great Greek thinkers, like the prophets, were Christians before Christ, and that it was the mission of Christ to bring to maturity and to fullness the intimations and revelations of God which all good men, anywhere and everywhere had ever had. The New Testament is unequivocal at this point. It says, "God, who at sundry times and in divers manners spake in times past by the prophets, hath in these last days spoken unto his by his Son."

I said that this issue was settled by the Church in the second century. That statement is hardly just. This issue has to be decided afresh in every age. Is Christianity something quite apart from all other insights into religion and all other revelations of God, or does it gather up into itself and fulfill insights often reached in the first instance by means quite apart from its distinctive truths. The latter, rather than the former, alternative is my own belief. Christianity, as I see it, takes up and carries on whatever sincere quests for God any man makes, under any conditions, and concedes the truth of whatever insights he may have sincerely achieved. Christianity does not deny the intimations of God which all of us get constantly from a hundred sources: science, art, history, and the like. But it does interpret them and mature them. Thus, I should like to leave with you a few words, spoken a generation ago by a great interpreter of Christianity, though not an apologist for any theory of special revelation, Josiah Royce:

Christianity stands before us as the most effective expression of religious longing which the human race, travailing in pain until now, has, in its corporate capacity, as yet, been able to bring before its imagination as a vision, or has endeavored to translate, by the labor of love, into the terms of its own real life. . . . The Christian religion is, thus far at least, man's most impressive vision of salvation, and his principal glimpse of the homeland of the spirit.[4]

[4] Josiah Royce, *The Problem of Christianity* (New York: The Macmillan Company, 1913), Vol. I, pp. 10, 11.

INDEX